P9-BZC-734

D0015362

Art of SEED BEADING

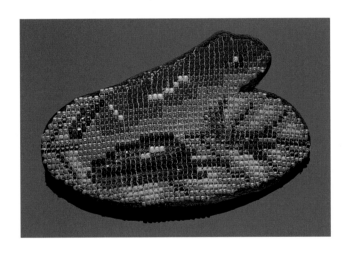

Elizabeth Gourley, Jane Davis
& Ellen Talbott

Sterling Publishing Co., Inc.
New York

For Mike, Amy, and Greg—E.G.

For Rich, Jeff, Andrew, and Jonathan—J.K.D.

For Alan, Walter, and George—E.T.

Library of Congress Cataloging-in-Publication Data

Gourley, Elizabeth.
    Art of seed beading / Elizabeth Gourley, Jane Davis & Ellen
Talbott.
        p.   cm.
    Includes index.
    ISBN 0-8069-7755-8
    1. Beadwork. I. Davis, Jane, 1959– . II. Talbott, Ellen. III. Title.
TT860.G68   1999
745.58'2—dc21   98-40844
                                                        CIP

10 9 8 7 6 5 4 3 2 1

Published by Sterling Publishing Company, Inc.
387 Park Avenue South, New York, N.Y. 10016
© 1999 by Elizabeth Gourley, Jane Davis & Ellen Talbott
Distributed in Canada by Sterling Publishing
c/o Canadian Manda Group, One Atlantic Avenue, Suite 105
Toronto, Ontario, Canada M6K 3E7
Distributed in Great Britain and Europe by Cassell PLC
Wellington House, 125 Strand, London WC2R 0BB, England
Distributed in Australia by Capricorn Link (Australia) Pty Ltd.
P.O. Box 6651, Baulkham Hills, Business Centre, NSW 2153, Australia
Printed in Hong Kong
All rights reserved

Sterling ISBN 0-8069-7755-8

CONTENTS

ACKNOWLEDGMENTS

———— ■ ————

We owe a debt of gratitude to many people without whom this book wouldn't have been possible:

Thank you, Sheila Barry, Acquisitions Manager at Sterling Publishing Co., Inc., for believing in us and giving us the chance to make our dreams come true.

Thank you, Hazel Chan and Wanda Kossak, for being so gracious in your job and making the editing of the book so painless.

Thank you, Myra Nunley and Myra's Photography Studio, Ventura, Calif., for the beautiful photos that make the book.

Thank you, David Nuck, for the invaluable computer help.

Thank you, Kathy Yeomans, for all the hours you spent editing.

Thank you, Carole Tripp from Creative Castle in Newbury Park, Calif., for letting us peruse your store and borrow what we needed for photographing, and for hours of sharing your beading expertise.

Thank you, Carolyn Villines from Spanish Moss Trading Company in Ojai, Calif., for the fascinating discussions on the sizes and history of beads and bead manufacturing.

Thank you, Mrs. Mayfield, Mr. and Mrs. Joe Hernandez, Corinne Loomer, for letting us photograph your beautiful antique purses.

Thank you to the Gourley family for putting up with the neglect while your mother beaded.

Thank you to the Talbott family for all their help with the computer and their willingness to get their own snacks after school and cooking dinner while I was busy working.

Thank you to the Davis family for living with too much fast food, Mom being always busy on the computer or "creating," and beads everywhere!

1

INTRODUCTION

There is something so appealing about stringing little bits of shining color together into an elegant glass fabric. A small treasure of detail and design. Dancing dangling fringes, the changing colors through the light, the iridescent surfaces. No doubt about it, stringing beads is a fun and addictive craft. Walking through a bead store takes a feat of self-control to curb the urge to buy at least one of everything in the store—not that there's any intended project at hand—just because they are all so pretty.

This book is for others like us who love working with detail and those sparkling beads, and have an eclectic urge to try it all. From peyote stitch, brick stitch, and loom work to bead knitting and crochet, it's all here to delve into and enjoy. Use it as a "how to" if you are a beginner or as a resource if you've already caught the beading bug. We hope this book will show you new techniques you haven't tried, provide a variety of projects to complete, spark your creativity, and inspire you to make your own designs. Above all, we want this book to be enjoyed for the fun and beauty of beadwork.

Manufacturing Seed Beads

As you look closely at the grains of sand on the beach, each grain's individuality becomes evident. Like the sands on the beach, each seed bead has its own personality, color variance, and shape. And it's no wonder, because beads are basically sand.

Seed beads have been manufactured for thousands of years—from the ancient Egyptians making faience beads to modern-day Japanese computer-run bead factories. But, on the whole, the method of making seed beads hasn't changed much over the centuries.

There are two main ways of making glass beads: the wound method and the drawn method. The wound bead method is one of the oldest techniques. It is not used any more for seed beads, because it is a very time-consuming method of making one bead at a time. Today, this method is used mainly for single ornamental beads.

For the wound bead technique, a glass rod must be made first by gathering a hunk of molten glass on an iron bar. This hunk of glass is called a gather. Then a second bar is inserted into the glass. Two workers, one on each bar, quickly run away from each other to create a glass rod, which can be sized in different diameters depending on how far and how quickly the glass is pulled apart. This rod quickly solidifies and is then cut into smaller rods for easy handling. One end of these smaller rods is heated up again and twisted around a wire. Once the rod is twisted all around the wire, it is cut off, and the ring left on the wire is reheated and shaped until it is smooth and round.

This is repeated on the same wire several times. The rings of glass or "beads" are then left to cool. When cooled, the beads can be easily slipped off the wire, which contracts more than the glass does.

Another form of the wound bead is the multiple wound bead. Many years ago, the capability to heat up a thick rod of glass to make a larger bead didn't exist. Thus, the multiple wound method was devised. In this method, the glass rods are wound around the wire several times, one upon the other, to make larger beads. Technology has updated some of these steps, but basically the wound method remains the same today as it was centuries ago.

The drawn bead technique is a better method for making large quantities of beads. Seed beads are now primarily made with this technique. There are several variations on the drawn bead technique. One of the older variations starts the same way as the wound bead technique— with a hunk of molten glass. An air bubble is formed in the middle of the hunk so that a tube forms when the glass is pulled, instead of a rod. This tube is cut into small pieces, which are then tumbled to smooth the edges.

It takes nearly 2 months to make a batch of drawn seed beads! A modern variation starts with a cauldron of the best quartz sand. The sand is heated in the cauldron for 21 days until it has reached its peak temperature of 2372–2732°F (1300–1500°C). The sand then turns to a molten liquid. At this stage, different chemicals, such as silica, cobalt, opaquants, bauxite, or even gold dust, are added according to the color or type of bead desired. After the liquid glass has reached its peak temperature, it is ladled by hand out of the cauldron into a smaller furnace. The glass is again heated and slowly turns into glass tube forms. When the tubes are ready, they are pulled out of the furnace with a pulley. The glass is pulled to a distance of 120 ft. (40 meters). This long tube is then cut into 3 ft. (1 meter) lengths. The speed of the pulling and the cooling of the glass at this stage determine the exterior size of the bead and its hole size. One 120-foot tube is comprised of several different-sized tubes. The parts of the tube that have been pulled farther are smaller in diameter than the parts of the tube closer to the furnace.

The 3-foot (1 meter) tubes are sized, cut into smaller pieces, then mixed with crushed charcoal, sand, and liquid plaster. This mixture is put into a furnace, which looks similar to a cement mixer, where it is heated to 1440°F (800°C) and rotated. This shrinks the small tubes to their round bead form. This is one of the most crucial steps in making a bead, because the heat has to be exactly right to ensure the correct roundness and color. At this stage, the color of the bead emerges. Before this, the molten glass had been colorless. Now the bead maker can tell if he has achieved the desired color of the bead.

The charcoal, sand, and plaster get stuck in the holes of the beads, which must then be shaken out. After the shaking process, the beads are cooled in a tumbler with sawdust. When the beads have been tumbled and cooled enough, they are cleaned and sorted by size. After 60 days this whole process starts all over again for every color.

Glass seed beads seem more precious and special when you understand the manufacturing process. Each seed bead is its own tiny work of art.

Sizes and Types of Beads

Beads come in a wide range of sizes, shapes, and finishes. The possibilities for more variety in beads has grown with each new technique in the manufacturing and finishing process. Although there are generally accepted names of finishes, sizes, and types of beads, there are also subtle variations depending on which manufacturer, retailer, or beader was consulted. The following is a basic description of the sizes, types, and finishes of beads.

Seed beads are round doughnut-shaped beads that range in size from the tiny size 24° , not much bigger

Bead sizes (left to right): 9mm (crow bead), 7mm (trade bead), 5°(pony bead), 6°, 8°, 9°, 10°, 11°, 12°, 13°, 15°, 18°, 19°, 20°, 22°.

than a grain of sand, through size 6°, a little larger than the size of a peppercorn. Seed beads smaller than size 15° have not been made since the 1890's and are antiques. Size 5° and sometimes size 6° beads are referred to as "pony beads" rather than seed beads. Trade beads or size 1° beads are the next larger size bead. The largest is called a crow bead. The actual size of a bead varies somewhat within a category, and beads made by different manufacturers can vary as much as a whole bead size.

The thin-walled Japanese *tubular beads* are called Delicas or Antiques. They come in size 11° (close to a size 13° or 14° in seed beads) and in a 3.3mm size (similar to a size 8° in seed beads). All projects in this book calling for Japanese tubular beads refer to the size 11° bead. These

beads, with their large holes and uniform shape, fit together like bricks, making them ideal for peyote and brick stitch projects.

Faceted beads are finished beads that have been ground to a flat surface on one or more sides. Seed beads with one facet ground into the side are called *charlottes. Two-cuts* look like short faceted bugle beads. *Three-cuts* are beads with random cuts all over. Cylindrical Japanese beads made from a six-sided cane of glass are called *hex-cuts.* Austrian *Swarovski crystals* are beads made from high-quality leaded glass and cut with precise facets like precious stones.

Bugle beads are longer slices of the same glass canes used for seed and Delica type beads. They can be 1/8 inch or longer. Twisted bugle beads are cut from five- or six-sided canes of glass that have been twisted while the glass was hot.

There are many other shapes of beads to use for accents and details in beadwork. *Drop beads* can look like a teardrop, or have a molded or pressed shape. They can have the hole drilled through the side at the small end of the bead or drilled vertically through the center. Pressed glass beads can be made into nearly any shape—from teardrops to flowers and leaves. *Bi-cone* beads look like two rounded cone shapes joined together at the wide end of the cone.

Lampwork beads were named because of the smaller torch used in their manufacturing, compared with the huge furnaces used for glass-blowing large items, such as plates

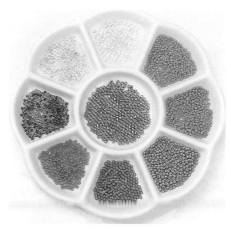

Bead types (clockwise from the dark blue on the top): Size 13° charlotte, blue iris finish; Size 11° opaque medium blue, pearl luster; 3.3mm Delica transparent, silver, AB finish; Size 11° Delica opaque, matte blue, AB finish; Hex-cut, opaque pale blue, glossy finish; Square cut, blue iris finish; Size 11° three-cut, raspberry, luster finish; Two-cut, pale blue, satin finish. Center: 2mm bugle, blue iris; 4mm bugle, matte blue AB finish; 12mm bugle, metallic pale blue.

Bead finishes (clockwise from the top): Size 8° transparent light blue, light blue lined, AB finish; Size 13° blue opaque matte; Size 13° blue opaque glossy; 11° blue opaque pearl luster; Size 12° blue white heart; Size 12° blue greasy; Size 11° transparent light blue, dark blue lined; Size 11° transparent pale blue, AB finish. Center: Size 11° rocaille, blue, silver-lined, square hole, AB finish.

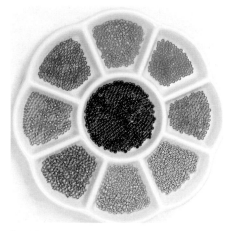

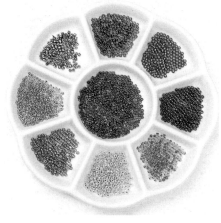

Bead finishes (clockwise from the top): Size 11° green metallic; Size 11° transparent amber, green lined; Size 11° rocaille, aqua, silver-lined, square hole; Size 11° light aqua, silver-lined, round hole; Size 11° transparent turquoise, glossy, AB finish; Size 11° transparent turquoise, matte, AB finish; Size 11° transparent turquoise, matte; Size 11° transparent turquoise, shiny. Center: Size 11° blue iris.

Bead finishes (clockwise from the top): Size 8° transparent light blue, light blue lined, AB finish; Size 13° blue opaque matte; Size 13° blue opaque glossy; 11° blue opaque pearl luster; Size 12° blue white heart; Size 12° blue greasy; Size 11° transparent light blue, dark blue lined; Size 11° transparent pale blue, AB finish. Center: Size 11° rocaille, blue, silver-lined, square hole, AB finish.

and glasses. Lampwork beads are made individually by melting the end of a glass rod onto a wire. Beads can be made uniform, after years of practice, or as individual art pieces and miniature sculptures.

The glass used to make a bead can be transparent, opaque, or a shade in between. The terms *greasy,*

opal, and *satin* refer to various properties of beads somewhere between transparent and opaque. *Greasy beads* are made of a cloudy-looking glass that is neither transparent nor opaque. *Opal beads* are similar to greasy beads though a little more transparent. *Satin beads* have tiny bubbles pulled into the glass to give

it a directional sheen. *White heart* beads are made from white canes with a thin coating of colored glass (made originally to conserve the costly colored glass) and look similar to greasy beads from the side.

A finished bead, in any of the glass types, can be dyed or painted to achieve the desired color. The hole in the bead can be lined with silver or another color, and can be square or round. A square hole gives lined beads with transparent or translucent glass more of a shimmer. Silver lined beads are sometimes called *Rocaille beads* (pronounced *row kie,* as in pie).

The surface of a bead can be shiny, matte, or semi-gloss. The bead can have hot metal salts baked on the surface to achieve a rainbow iridescence. These are called *aurora borealis, AB, rainbow,* or *iris* beads. *Iris beads* are usually opaque black or very dark opaque beads with the metal salts coating. A *luster finish* is a clear or transparent colored coating that gives the bead a clear or transparent colored shine. Beads with a pearlescent look usually have a milky luster, and have pearl or Ceylon in their name. *Galvanized beads* have a thin metal coating electroplated to the surface of the bead. *Metallic beads* usually refer to any bead with a metallic look, which can either have a baked-on paint or be galvanized.

Finishes, such as painted metallics, dyed beads, some pearlescent finishes, and bead hole linings, are sometimes easily worn off with wear. Testing a sample of beads by soaking them in bleach or alcohol can help determine if the color or finish will likely last. Spraying the beads with a clear acrylic finish can help make these beads more durable.

A bead can have a different visual effect, depending on the type of glass used in its making, any facets ground into its surface, and the type of finish applied to its surface or hole. Combinations of these properties give us the great variety of bead choices in our projects.

Beading Tools and Supplies

Beading requires few tools and supplies. Here is a list of the basics: needles, thread, scissors, pliers, beeswax, trays and containers, glue and nail polish, a bead loom, findings, and wire.

■ Needles

Beading needles are thin and straight with very small eyes. This can make threading the needle a bit of a challenge. A helpful hint is to cut your thread at an angle before you try to thread the needle.

The needles are sized according to their length and thickness. There are short needles (1 1/4 inches long), long needles (2 inches long), and loom needles (3 inches long). Most beading needles come in sizes #10, #11, #12, #13, #15, and #16. Size #10 needles are the thickest and size #16 are the thinnest. The numbers approximately correspond to bead sizes. Size #10's are usually good for size 9–10 beads, size #12's are good for beads 11 and 12, and size #15's

are good for 14, 15, and smaller beads. Since beading needles can break and bend easily, it is a good idea to have a ready supply.

Use twisted wire and Big Eye needles for stringing beads on the thick thread used for knitting and crocheting beads. Twisted wire needles have large, collapsible eyes and come in sizes #6 ultra thin, #10 medium, and #12 heavy. They are made of a thin wire twisted together. They do not have a sharp point; therefore, they are not good for embroidery or leatherwork. It is very easy to thread Big Eye needles, because their eye runs down the entire length of the needle except for the two points at either end.

To do the knitting projects in this book, you will also need knitting needles. The knitting needles used for beadwork are very thin, double-pointed needles. They come in sizes 00–000000, with 00 being the thicker needles and 000000 being the thinnest.

The small, steel crochet hooks needed for crocheting with beads are sizes US 7–13.

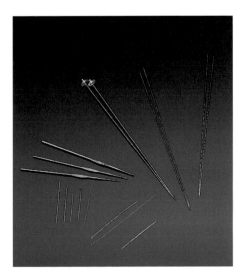

A variety of needles

■ Thread

Nylon, kevlar, linen, silk, and cotton are some of the fibers used to make beading thread. Nymo thread is nylon thread that ranges in size from 000, 00, 0, A, B, C, D, E, F, FF to FFF. The smallest size is 000 and the largest size is FFF. The size of the thread to use will depend on the size of the bead you are using. Size D thread is a good size to start with, as it works well with size 11° beads. Nymo thread comes in different colors and looks a bit like dental floss. It is good for loom weaving, off-loom weaving, and embroidery.

Silk thread comes in several different colors and gauges (thin, medium, and thick sizes). It is good thread for stringing necklaces, knotting, knitting, and crochet.

Kevlar thread is thin and very strong. It is available in a size similar to size 0 Nymo thread. It is available only in black or beige, but it is good to use when strength is essential.

French linen thread is 100% linen. It comes in two sizes: #60 fine (good for use with beads 13°, 14°, 16°, and 18°) and #100 medium (good

Assortment of beading thread (top to bottom): cotton cord, size 5; cotton cord, size 8; cotton cord, size 12; nylon, size F; nylon, size D; nylon, size B; nylon, size O; nylon, size OO

Beading threads come in many colors.

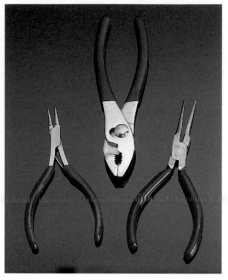
Pliers (left to right): round needlenose, pliers, needlenose

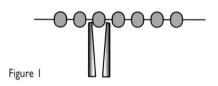
Figure I

Beeswax and thread conditioner

for use with beads 8°, 10°, 11° and 12°).

Perle cotton thread is used for knitting and crocheting with beads. It is 100% cotton and available in sizes #50–#3. The smaller the number, the thicker the size. Most bead knitting uses size #8.

■ Scissors

Scissors are an essential tool. Small, sharp-pointed embroidery scissors are the best for doing the close work needed in beading.

Small pointed embroidery scissors work best for beadwork.

■ Pliers

Small pliers or needle-nosed pliers are used for breaking unwanted beads on your thread. For instance, if you threaded on one too many green beads and you don't want to undo all the beads you've threaded on after it, you can break the unwanted green bead with the pliers. Make sure your eyes are covered so that the flying glass won't hurt you.

Break the bead as shown in Fig. 1, or else you might break the thread as well. You can also break the bead by forcing a large sewing needle through the hole of the bead.

Pliers are also used to pull your needle through a bead with a small hole, or one that has been packed full of thread. Be careful not to pull too hard, as some beads have been known to break from the pressure. Round needle-nosed pliers are used to bend wire.

■ Beeswax

Beeswax strengthens and protects your thread and helps keep it from tangling. Before threading beads, just run your thread through the beeswax, then pull the thread through your fingers to remove excess wax. A thread conditioner called Thread Heaven is also available.

■ Trays and Canisters

Trays are essential for spreading out your beads while you work so that you can easily pick them up with your needle and for inspecting your beads to determine the bad ones from the good. Plastic divided plates, pie tins, plastic or ceramic watercolor palettes and mixing trays, or any type of shallow container will work just fine. Make sure your tray is plain white or a light color so that you can see the beads easier. If you're working with light-colored beads, a darker color tray will work best.

You will also need containers for storing your beads. Some can be stored in the original tube or small ziplock bag that they come in. Other beads, which come in hanks or little plastic bags that have to be cut open, will need a storage container. You can buy empty tubes or small ziplock

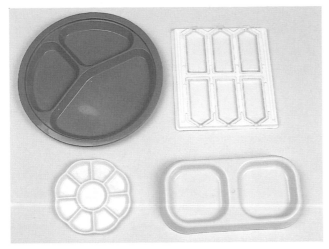

Bead trays

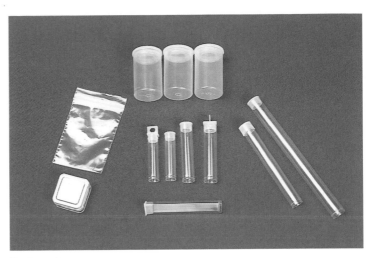

Bead containers

bags, or you can use little jars or plastic bottles that you may find around your house. We like to use empty 35mm film canisters because they are easy to open, consistent in size, and they're always lying around. Plus, we hate to just throw them away. The fairly transparent ones are the best to use because you can see what's inside.

■ Glue

You will need a good, strong glue when adhering your beadwork to fabric, leather, wood, or whatever material you're working on. Leather

A strong, waterproof glue is important for adhering beadwork to fabric, leather, or wood. Nail polish painted on the end of thread can be used like a needle. It's also good for securing knots.

Weld™ and Weld Bond™ are two products that work very well. There are also many other glues available. Whichever you choose, make sure that it is strong, waterproof, and fast-drying.

■ Findings and Wire

Ear wires, clasps, barrettes, and handbag frames are used for some of the projects in this book. You can also bead on wire. Wire is sized by its gauge ranging from 10–28 (using even numbers). Ten-gauge is the thickest and heaviest wire, and 28-gauge is the thinnest. Wire comes in different shapes, such as triangular, square, and half-round, and in different pliabilities. The projects in this book use round wires that are 20-gauge and 24-gauge.

■ Bead Looms

There are several different bead looms on the market today that range in price from inexpensive to somewhat expensive. Most bought looms are designed for narrow, long projects, such as belts and head-bands. If you are going to make a wider project, you will probably have

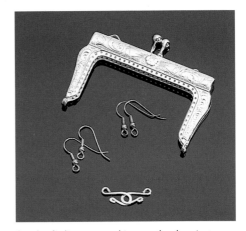

Jewelry findings are used in many bead projects.

Wire cutters and wire

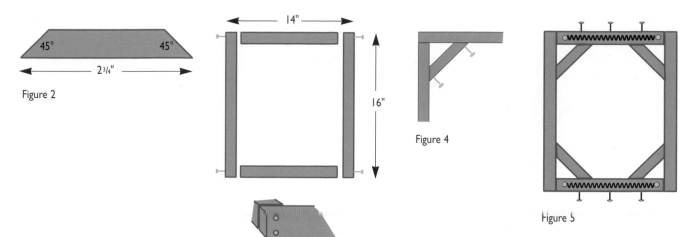

45°   45°

2³/₄"

Figure 2

14"

16"

Figure 3

Figure 4

Figure 5

Homemade and store-bought bead looms

to make your own loom. But don't worry! Making a loom is very easy. You can vary its size according to the size of your project. There are several different types of looms that you can make. The following loom works for most of the loomed projects in this book:

MATERIALS:

Six linear feet of 1 x 2 pine
Twenty-four 1¹/₄-inch finishing nails
Ten 1¹/₄-inch common nails
Two 8- or 9-inch springs about ¹/₂
    inch in diameter (We prefer sturdy
    springs. The ones we use have 126
    coils. You will need one with at
    least 80 coils.)

Cut the pine into two 16-inch lengths and two 14-inch lengths. Use the remaining lumber to cut four 2³/₄-inch-long pieces to use as braces. Cut the ends of the braces at 45° angles using a miter box. See Fig. 2. Nail the two 16-inch lengths to the two 14-inch lengths as shown in Fig. 3. Next, nail the four braces to the inside corners of the loom for added strength. See Fig. 4. Next, nail the springs to the 1-inch side of the 14-inch 1 x 2's, stretching the springs slightly, so there is room for your warp threads to fit between the coils. Make sure your springs are both on the front side of the loom. Hammer three nails, evenly spaced, at either end of the loom, leaving about ¹/₂ inch of the nails sticking out. See Fig. 5.

You can also use a plain wooden picture frame as the base of the loom. Remove the glass, nail the springs to the front of opposite ends, then hammer in three nails to the sides of the top and bottom of the frame, leaving about ¹/₂ inch of the nails sticking out.

2

TECHNIQUES

Abbreviations

PNT: Pass the needle through
PNBT: Pass the needle back through
PNDT: Pass the needle down through
PNUT: Pass the needle up through
SC: Single crochet
K: Knit
KB: Knit bead
P: Purl
PB: Purl bead
inc1: Knit or purl into front and back of the same stitch (increase)
psso: Pick up the second stitch and pull it over the first stitch (decrease)
s1: Slip a stitch
tog: Together

There are many techniques for stitching beads together, and each technique can be accomplished using several different methods. The following are methods we used for the projects in this book.

Bead Weaving: Needle and Loom Techniques

■ Peyote Stitch

Peyote stitch, or gourd stitch, has been used for beading by Native Americans for hundreds of years. Some tribes reserve the term "peyote" stitch for projects sacred to their culture and refer to all else as gourd stitch. It is a simple, versatile stitch with many nuances.

The basic stitch begins by stringing a length of beads that will become the first two rows of the project. Begin the third row, which organizes the first three rows when complete, by stringing one bead, then passing the needle back through the third bead from the needle towards the tail end of the thread, and pulling tight. See Photo 1. This lines up two beads vertically on top of each other at the end of the row, and the next bead halfway between.

To continue, string one bead, skip one bead, pass the needle through the next bead, pull tight. See Photo 2. This creates a pattern of two beads vertically on top of each other and one bead stepped between.

The stitch is continued on each new row by always positioning the thread so that it is coming out of one of the upper beads, then by stringing one bead, skipping the bead that is stepped down half a space, and passing the needle through the next bead that is stepped up half a space. See Photo 3. Pull the thread tight to fit the bead in place. See Photo 4. Each row is made up of every other bead along a horizontal line.

Counting Rows: To count the rows, begin at one corner of the piece, or graph, and count diagonally or in a zigzag fashion so that you count every row.

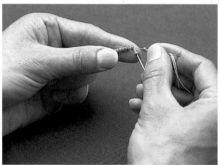

Photo 3

Photo 4

Peyote stitch with size 11° seed beads

Photo 1

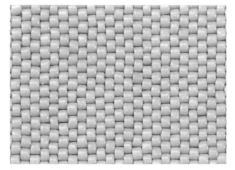

Photo 2

Peyote stitch with Delica beads

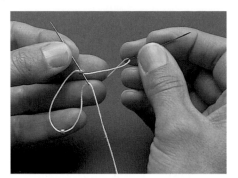

Photo 5

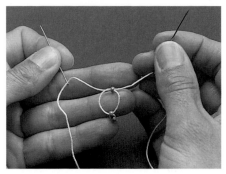

Photo 6

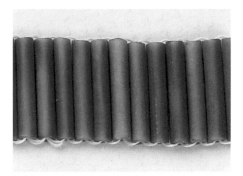

Ladder stitch with bugle beads

Peyote stitch has many idiosyncrasies and variations. Entire books have been written that delve into all the details of this stitch. Our book is meant to be a sampling of many ways to make fabric with beads, and so we do not cover all the nuances of each technique. However, here are two interesting things to be aware of about peyote for the projects in this book.

The Odd Count Turnaround: When beginning with an uneven number of beads in a flat project, you will always have to pass the needle through several beads at the end of the row on one side of the piece in order to get the thread in the proper position to add the next bead on the new row.

That Shifty First Bead: In circular peyote, when you add the last bead in a round, you need to pass the needle through the first bead in that round to prepare for the next round. This moves the first bead in each round over by one bead. A diagonal line on the graph indicates the first bead in each round. However, some people stitch with the developing piece below them. Others stitch with the developing piece above them. The diagonal line for the first stitch in each round is reversed, depending on which stitching method is used and in which direction you stitch.

Circular peyote stitch patterns in this book show a diagonal line from the top left to bottom right for stitching right to left, with the work below, as in the how-to photos in this section.

■ Ladder Stitch

The ladder stitch is used to make a base for the brick stitch (see next stitch). Bugle beads are usually used for this stitch, but you can also use seed beads. You will need two beading needles for this stitch. First, thread each end of a length of thread with a beading needle. Then string one bead and position it in the middle of the thread. Pick up another bead and PNT one end of the bead. Then use the other needle and PNT the opposite end of the bead. See Photo 5. Pull tight until the second bead is positioned next to the first bead in the middle of the thread. See Photo 6. Continue in this manner until you reach the desired length. To form the ladder of beads into a circular shape, pass each needle through opposite ends of the first bead in the ladder. Pull tight.

■ Brick Stitch

A project done in the brick stitch looks similar to a brick wall—hence, its name. The beads lie in a vertical position, and the stitch is usually worked in the round. To work the brick stitch, you must first have a ladder-stitch base (see previous stitch).

Pick up two beads with your needle, then stick the needle under a loop of thread that is connecting the first pair of beads on the ladder stitch base. See Photo 7. Then PNBT the second bead strung and pull tight. See Photos 8 and 9. *String one bead. PNT loop of thread that is connecting the next pair of beads. See

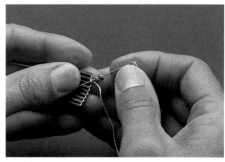

Photo 7

Photo 8

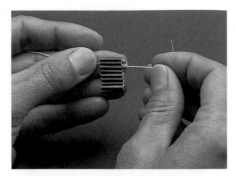

Photo 9

Photo 10

Photo 11

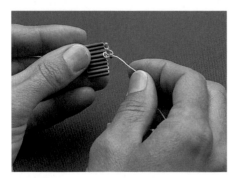

Photo 12

Brick stitch with size 11° seed beads

Brick stitch with Delica beads

Photo 10. PNBT the bead and pull tight. See Photos 11 and 12.* Repeat between asterisks until the end of the round. To finish a row when working in the round, PNDT the first bead in the row and back up through the second bead.

■ Herringbone Stitch

The herringbone stitch, which originated in Africa, gives the finished project a beautiful woven or knitted look. There are two methods of beginning the herringbone stitch. Here is the one we used in this book. After mastering the first few rows, it is an easy stitch to do. This stitch is best used for flat pieces. You must have at least four beads per row, or a number divisible by four, because the herringbone stitch is done in groups of two with single beads on each end. For this example, we will use twelve-bead rows. Always keep the thread tension tight, except in Row 1, where you can adjust the stitches evenly.

ROW 1: String twelve beads. String one more bead. PNT the #12 bead. Skip the next two beads (#11 and #10). PNT the next bead, #9. String two beads. PNT next bead, #8. Skip the next two beads (#7 and #6). PNT the next bead, #5. String two beads. PNT the next bead, #4. Skip the next two beads (#3 and #2). PNT the last bead.

ROW 2: String two beads. PNBT first bead strung. See Photo 13. Skip next bead. See Fig. 1. String two beads. PNT next bead. *Skip one bead. PNT next bead. See Fig. 2. String two beads. PNT next bead.* Repeat between asterisks until end of row. Every other two-bead set will be hanging down. Since these were the two beads skipped in the first row, they must be pushed up above the thread so that they are ready for the needle to pass through them. This only happens on Row 2.

ROW 3: String two beads. PNBT first bead strung. *PNT the first bead of the next two-bead set. See Photo 14.

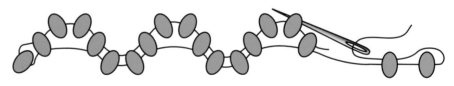

Figure 1

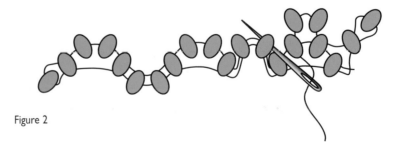

Figure 2

Photo 13

Photo 14

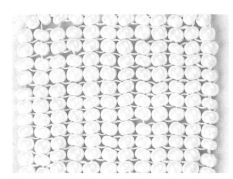

Herringbone stitch with size 10° seed beads

Photo 15

Photo 16

Herringbone stitch with Delica beads

String two beads. PNT the last bead of the two-bead set. See Photo 15.* Repeat between asterisks until end of row.

ROW 4: Same as Row 3.

As you have probably noticed by now, the beads of each row are not in a straight line. Each group of two makes an inverted U-shape. When pulling your stitches tight, especially with matte Japanese tubular beads, make sure one bead is on one side of the "U" and one is on the other. See Photo 16.

ENDING ROW
There are two different ending rows used in the projects in this book. One makes the edge even. The other makes the edge look the same as the beginning edge—singular beads topping each group of two beads.

Even Edge: String one bead. PNT next two beads of two-bead set. *String one bead. PNT next two beads of two-bead set.* Repeat between asterisks until end of row.

To make both ends look the same, turn piece over and do the same thing to the beginning edge.

Singular Bead Topping: String two beads. PNT first bead of previous row. String one bead. *PNT next two beads. String one bead.* Repeat between asterisks until end of row.

■ Square Stitch

Beads worked in the square stitch have a very similar appearance to loomed work. It is sometimes called the false loom weave stitch. To do the square stitch, start by stringing the desired amount of beads on your thread. Do not make a knot at the end of your thread, because the tension of the thread may need to be adjusted. If the tension of the thread is too tight, your work might curl. For the second row, string two beads, then PNBT second-to-last bead on the first row in the opposite direction. See Photo 17. Then PNBT the second bead on Row 2. See Photo 18.

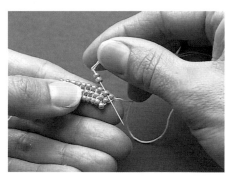

Photo 17

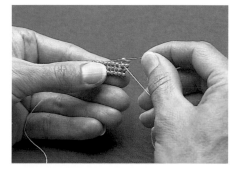

Photo 18

Photo 19

Photo 20

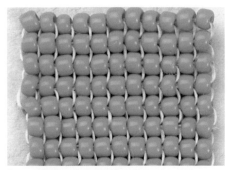

Square stitch with size 11° seed beads

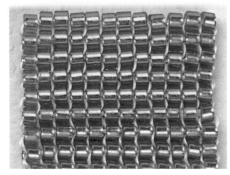

Square stitch with Delica beads

String a bead and PNT third bead from the last on the first row in the opposite direction. See Photo 19. Then PNBT third bead on second row in the same direction as the row. See Photo 20. Continue in this manner, adding on one bead at a time until the end of row. At the beginning of each row, add on two beads at a time.

■ Netting

Netting is a quick way to cover a surface with beads. Made up of interconnected loops of beads rather than single beads stitched right next to each other, netting allows both speed in the making and more variety in the surface texture than many other stitches. The loops can be made using accent beads or combining different sizes of beads to create new effects. The finished fabric can be open and lacy, or close and dense. The size and spacing of the loop repeat determines the density of the finished fabric. Although netting can be made in any color combination, it is most easily accomplished when the bead that links the loops together is a different color from the other beads in the fabric.

To make a sample of netting, string twelve beads. String three beads, skip four beads, PNT the next one (the eighth bead). See Photo 21. String three beads. Skip three beads. PNT the fourth one. See Photo 22. Pull tight. See Photo 23. Second row and all other rows thereafter: String three beads. PNT the next bead (top bead of three-bead loop). See Photo 24.

The following are instructions for a sample of circular netting. The white beads are the links between the loops.

ROUND 1: String three green beads and one white bead. Repeat nine times. Tie the tail end and working end of the thread into a circle with a square knot.

ROUND 2: String two green beads, one white bead, two green beads, and PNT the next white bead on the first round. Repeat all the way around.

ROUND 3: PNT the first three beads in Round 2. The needle will be coming out of a white bead. Repeat Round 2.

Continue repeating Round 3 for as long as you wish the tube to be. To increase the diameter of the tube, string three or more green beads instead of two in each side of each loop. To decrease, string fewer green beads on each side of each loop. This way, the netting can hug the surface of a container or flatten out into a circle.

Flat netting is the same principle as circular netting, except the rows are completed back and forth. More beads need to be strung at the begin-

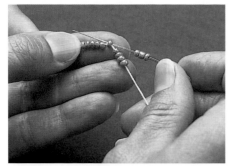

Photo 21

Photo 22

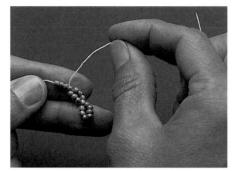

Photo 23

Photo 24

Netting in size 11° seed beads

Netting in Delica beads

ning of each row to account for the edge of the net, and you must pass through some beads at the end of the rows to get the needle in the proper position for the following row.

The thread can make a difference in netting. Netting made flat tends to stay bunched up vertically unless you use thread almost the width of the bead hole rather than thin nylon beading thread. Silk, linen, or cotton cord are good choices. What thread you use is not as critical for netting that is intended to hug a surface.

■ Loom Bead Weaving

Loom bead weaving requires two sets of threads. They are the warp threads and the weft threads. The warp threads are the vertical threads that are supported by the loom. The weft thread carries the beads and runs horizontally.

WARPING THE LOOM

Before you can begin your loomed project, you must first attach the warp threads to the loom. To calculate the length of the warp threads,

take the finished length of your project and add 12 inches for finishing the work and another 12 inches for tying to the loom. If you wish to have fringe on your finished project, add the length of the fringe on both sides and double it. You will need one more warp thread than the number of beads in the width of your design. For example; if you have five beads across in your design, you will need six warp threads.

There are two ways to warp your loom, depending on the length of your project and the kind of loom you are using. Some looms are equipped with rollers at either end that you can loosen and tighten with wing nuts. If you are doing a project that is longer than the loom and your loom has rollers, calculate how long to make your warp threads and how many you will need. Then cut the desired length and number of warp threads and tie one end of the group of warp threads to one or more tack heads on the roller at the top of the loom. Loosen the roller and wind up the warp threads while holding the other end of the warp threads in one hand and keeping the threads taut. Continue winding until there is just enough thread left to tie the warp threads to the tack heads on the bottom of the loom. Before tying the warp threads to the bottom of the loom, line up the threads in the spring coils at both the top and bottom of the loom. Tie the warp ends to the tack heads on the bottom roller.

Next, decide where you want to start your weaving on the warp threads. Leave enough space on the warp threads at the beginning to use later for fringe and/or finishing your project. You may need to wind your warp thread from top to bottom until you reach the desired measurement. To do this, loosen both top and bot-

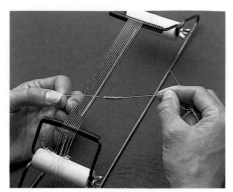

Photo 25

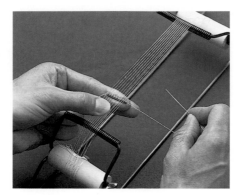

Photo 26

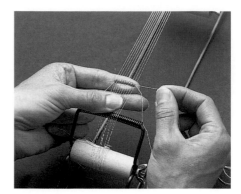

Photo 27

tom rollers and wind both at the same time while keeping the warp threads taut, but not too tight. Tighten the wing nuts. Remember that you will be weaving from the bottom of the loom to the top. Start weaving about 1 or 2 inches from the bottom coils.

When your project is smaller than your loom and you don't need lots of thread for fringe, you can warp your loom by making a loop knot at the end of the thread on the spool. Hook this loop over a nail or tack head at the top end of the loom. Calculate how wide your project will be and where to start the warp threads so that the work will be centered on the loom. Then line up the warp thread through the top spring coil and bring it down to the corresponding coil at the bottom spring. Wrap the thread around the nail or tack head at the bottom of the loom and take the thread up through the coil right next to the one you just used, bringing it up to the top of the loom and placing the thread into the corresponding coil. Next, loop it around the nail head again. Continue back and forth in this manner, keeping an even tension on the threads until you have the proper amount of warp threads on the loom. Then tie off the thread end to a nail head with your favorite knot. Cut the thread from the spool.

WEAVING

After warping your thread, you can begin weaving. When you start your weaving, remember to leave enough space at the beginning of the warp threads for finishing and tying off your work. Cut the desired length of weft thread (we like to use about 2 yards) and pass through beeswax. Thread the needle and tie the end of the weft thread to the left outside warp thread with an overhand knot, leaving about a 6-inch tail. See Photo 25. If you are left-handed, you will tie the end of the weft thread to the right outside warp thread and reverse all following instructions.

String desired number and color of beads according to the design chart. Read the chart from left to right and from bottom to top.

When stringing the beads for loom work, it is crucial to pick beads that are the same size and not irregular. Seed beads can vary dramatically in size and shape. If the beads are not the same size, your work will take on a very uneven appearance.

Now take the beads on the weft thread and place them under the warp threads. Push the beads up with your left index finger so there is a warp thread on both sides of each bead. See Photo 26. The first row or two can be tricky, but after that, the warp threads will hold the beads in place while you pass your needle

through the beads. Then, PNBT the beads, going from right to left. Make sure the holes of the beads are pushed up above warp threads so the needle goes back through beads above the warp threads. See Photo 27. If your needle goes under the warp threads, the beads will not be secured. If your needle goes through the warp threads, you won't be able to adjust the bead row up or down, which you may need to do. See Fig. 3. Continue in this manner, following the design chart.

When you have about 5 inches of weft thread left on your needle at the end of a row, it is time to get new thread. Take the needle off the thread and leave the tail of thread hanging for now. You will weave it in later. Thread the needle with new thread and PNT the last three or more rows of beads, making sure that the needle and thread end at the 5-inch tail. This will secure the new thread. Continue beading with the new thread. After you have made three or more new rows, thread the 5-inch tail and PNT the three or more new rows. Cut off excess thread. Weave in the beginning tail the same way.

FINISHING

When you come to the end of your project, there are several different ways to finish, depending on your project and your style. We will dis-

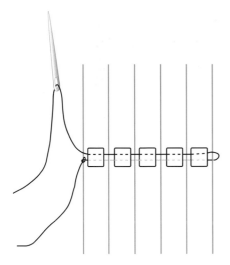

Figure 3

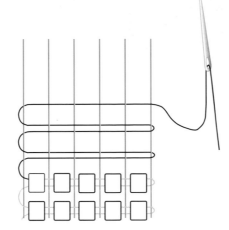

Figure 4

Figure 5

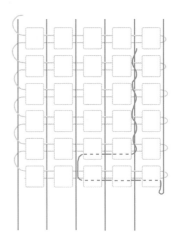

Figure 6

cuss three different ways to finish your project.

For a project where the back of the work will not show and there won't be any fringe, use your weft thread without any beads on it to weave several rows at the ending edge of the work and at the beginning edge. This will create a thread cloth that you will fold down to the back of the work and glue or sew in place. Take the needle and go under, over, under, over the warp threads until you reach the end of the row. For the next row, take the needle over, under, over, under the warp threads to the end. See Fig. 4. After making the thread cloth at the end of the project, go back to the beginning of the work and add a new weft thread. Weave several rows without beads to create a thread cloth at the beginning of work. Now remove the work from the loom and tie the pairs of warp threads together using a surgeon's knot. See Fig. 5. Continue until all warp threads have been tied. Trim threads and fold to the back of the work and glue or sew in place.

For projects where the front and back of the work are equally important, and you don't want fringe, the finishing is different. Don't make the thread cloth ends. Instead, remove

the finished work from the loom and weave each warp thread back into the body of the work. Do this by threading a needle with the warp thread and passing the needle and thread through several rows of beads. Do not pack the beads too full of threads as the beads can break from the pressure. When the beads get packed too full, take the remainder of the warp threads and wrap them back up the warp threads. See Fig. 6.

For projects that have fringed edges, remove the work from the loom and use the warp thread ends to create the fringe. Thread a warp thread with a needle and string the desired amount of beads on it. Skipping the last bead, PNBT the rest of the beads to the edge of the work. See Fig. 7. Make a double half-hitch knot near the edge of work. See Fig. 8. Weave the excess thread back into the body of the work by wrapping it

Figure 8

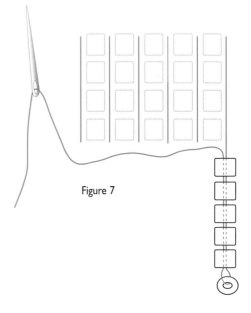

Figure 7

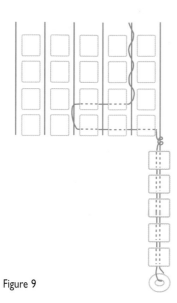

Figure 9

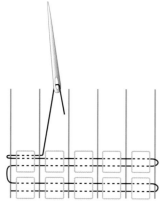

Figure 10

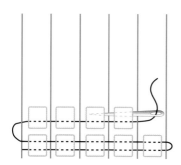

Figure 11

Loom bead weaving with size 11° seed beads

Loom bead weaving with Delica beads

around the warp threads and going through the beads. See Fig. 9. Be creative! There will be lots of warp ends to weave in and not much space to do it. It can be discouraging, but don't give up. It will be over before you know it!

DECREASING IN LOOM WORK
To decrease in loom work at the beginning of a row, go to the end of the row preceding the row that you wish to decrease and take the needle back through the number of beads to be decreased. Make sure to pass the weft thread under the outermost warp thread before going back through beads. Bring the weft thread to the back of the work and start the next row as you normally would. See Fig. 10. To decrease at the end of a row, add desired amount of beads and, ignoring excess warp thread, take needle to back of work and continue as you normally would. See Fig. 11.

Pre-strung Bead Techniques

■ Bead Knitting

There are several types of knitting with beads pre-strung onto thread. The projects in this book use bead knitting in plaited stockinette stitch, where each bead is pushed into the stitch as the stitch is made. There are

no beads on the wrong side of the fabric, and the beads on the right side of the fabric sit close together to cover the whole surface. In plaited stockinette stitch, the beads slant to the left on the right side of the knit row and slant to the right on the right side of the purl row. This way, they fit together neatly in a zigzag pattern, and the fabric doesn't bias.

In bead knitting, the tension needs to be tight in order to lock the beads in the stitches on the right side of the fabric. It helps to wrap the thread around a finger several times with about five or ten beads between the knitting and your hand. This way, you can slide a bead into place for the next stitch without having to let go of the right needle.

To make a sample of bead knitting, string about sixty-four size 8° seed beads onto size 5 perle cotton. Use a Big Eye needle to string the beads, or thread a size 10 beading needle with nylon or strong quilting thread, and tie it in a square knot around the perle cotton. Cast on twenty stitches to size 0 knitting needles.

ROW 1: Knit one row without beads. You make a plaited knit stitch by inserting the knitting needle in the back of the stitch and wrapping the thread around the right needle clockwise before completing the stitch.

ROW 2: Purl the next row without beads. You make a standard purl stitch by inserting the needle into the

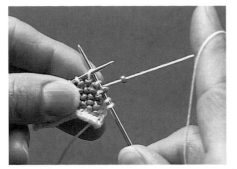

Photo 28

Photo 29

Photo 30

Photo 31

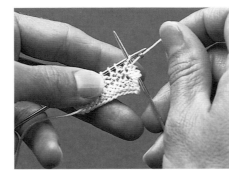

Photo 32

Photo 33

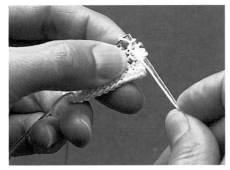

Photo 34

Bead knitting with size 11° seed beads

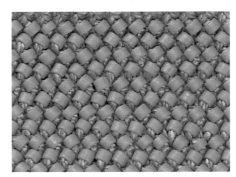

Bead knitting with Delica beads

front of the stitch and wrapping the thread around the right needle counterclockwise.

ROW 3: Knit two stitches in plaited knit stitch (as explained in Row 1), then insert the needle into the back of the next stitch and slide one bead about 1/2" away from the knitting. See Photo 28. Wrap the thread with the bead clockwise around the right needle and slide the bead down to the junction between the two needles. See Photo 29. At this point, pull the left needle towards you and the right needle away from you to create

a space between the stitch in progress. Now push the bead through the opening where the right needle will go to make the knit stitch. See Photo 30 (blue bead in this photo for clarity). Pull the needle through and complete the stitch. See Photo 31. Repeat the plaited bead knit stitch fifteen more times, then make two plaited knit stitches without beads.

ROW 4: Purl the first two stitches (as explained in Row 2), then insert the needle into the front of the next stitch, and slide one bead about 1/2" away from the knitting. See Photo 32.

Wrap the thread with the bead counterclockwise around the right needle and slide the bead down to the junction between the two needles. See Photo 33. This time, pull the right needle towards you and the left needle away from you to create a space in the stitch. Push the bead through the opening where the right needle will go to complete the purl stitch. Now push the right needle through and finish the stitch. See Photo 34. Repeat the bead purl stitch fifteen more times, then purl the last two stitches without beads.

Photo 35

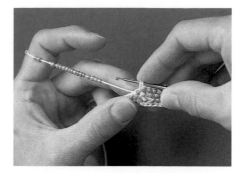

Photo 36

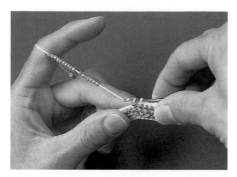

Photo 37

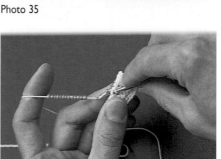

Photo 38

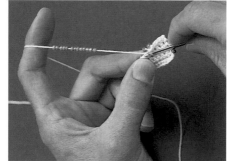

Photo 39

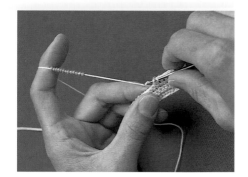

Photo 40

Bead crochet with Delica beads

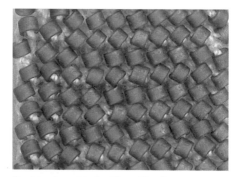

Bead crochet with size 8° seed beads

Repeat rows 3 and 4 until you are comfortable with bead knitting. More beads can be added by cutting the perle cotton about 2 feet (or more) away from the knitting and stringing the beads onto that end.

To bead knit using smaller beads and needles, the only variation is to slide the bead about 1/4" to 3/8" away from the knitting before wrapping the thread around the needle to make the stitch.

■ Crochet

The flat crochet method used in this book allows the beads to come out on the same side of the piece for each row.

Before you begin to crochet, string the beads to be used on the project onto the thread in the desired pattern. After the beads have been strung on, begin to crochet. Start crocheting with a simple chain stitch row of cotton thread. When you have chained as many stitches as

desired, do one row of SC without beads.

ROW 2: Start SC by sticking hook under top of stitch from previous row (two strands). Grab thread and pull through. See Photo 35. You now have two loops on the hook. Slide a bead down and push the bead with your fingers through the hole (in the top of the stitch from the previous row) where you just brought your hook through. See Photo 36. Then finish stitch by grabbing thread and pulling it through both loops on the hook. See Photo 37. Repeat this stitch until the end of the row. The beads will be on the front of the piece.

ROW 3: This row is easier than Row 2. The beads will appear on the back of the piece, which is really the front of the piece. Stick the hook under the top of the stitch from the previous row (two strands). Slide a bead down until it hits the piece. Grab the thread with the hook, making sure that the bead is caught between the hook and the piece. See Photo 38. Pull the thread through. See Photo 39. Now there are two loops on the hook, and the bead is attached behind the stitch. Finish the stitch by grabbing the thread and pulling it through both loops. See Photo 40. Repeat this stitch until the end of the row.

Repeat Rows 2 and 3 until desired length.

■ Tubular Beaded Crochet

Tubular beaded crochet is one of the simplest techniques to master for anyone who likes to crochet. The tube is made of slip stitches that spiral up, forming a cord, while the beads are simply held at the base of the thread before each loop is pulled through to complete the slip stitch. By varying the types and sizes of beads, or the thread thickness, you can create many different effects. The thicker the thread used in relation to the bead size, the more space will show up between the beads.

To make a practice sample of this technique, string four colors of size 8 beads on size 5 perle cotton in the sequence of one bead in color 1, one bead in color 2, one bead in color 3, and one bead in color 4. Repeat this same sequence about ten to twenty times. Make a slip knot. Then, using a size 7 crochet hook, make four bead chains by sliding a bead into each chain stitch as it is made. See Photos 41–43.

Begin the spiral by making a beaded slip stitch into the first beaded chain stitch you made. To do this, put the crochet hook through the beaded loop of the first chain stitch,

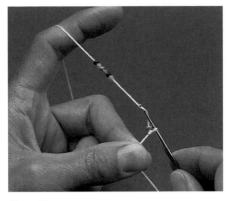
Photo 41

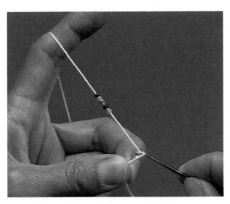
Photo 42

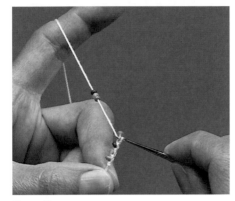
Photo 43

keeping the bead to the right of the hook. See Photo 44. Slide a new bead down the thread so it is behind, and to the right of, the bead on the loop. The new bead will be the same color as the bead on the loop the crochet hook is through. Wrap the thread over the crochet hook and pull it through both loops. See Photo 45 and Fig. 12. The new bead will be locked in the stitch to the right of the bead below. Continue in this manner by making a beaded slip stitch in every stitch. Every stitch you put the hook through will have the same color bead as the stitch you are making. The bead colors will spiral around the cord.

Figure 12

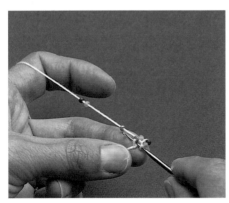
Photo 44

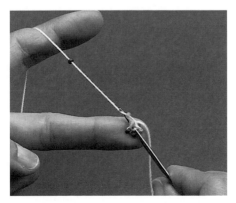
Photo 45

Tubular crochet with Delica beads

Tubular crochet with size 11° seed beads

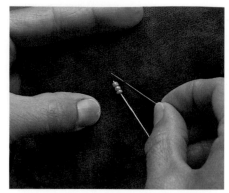

Photo 46

Photo 47

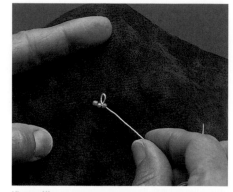

Photo 48

Backstitch

Embellishment Techniques

■ Backstitch

The backstitch is an excellent way to embellish fabric with beads. It is an embroidery stitch that attaches lines of beads to fabric, felt, or leather.

Knot a length of beading thread and PNUT back of fabric. *String one to three beads. The straighter the line, the more beads you use. PNDT fabric, then PNUT fabric at a point in between the last two beads strung. See Photo 46. PNBT the last bead strung. See Photo 47. Pull tight. See Photo 48.* Repeat between asterisks on entire area to be covered with beads.

■ Couching

Couching is a type of appliqué work where a string of beads is sewn onto fabric. Beads are strung on one needle and sewn down with another. Thread two needles and make a knot at the end of each thread. Push one needle up through the fabric and string on a length of beads. Push up the other needle from the bottom to the top of the fabric and tack down the thread of the bead strand. See Photo 49. Push the working needle back down through the fabric on the other side of the bead strand thread. See Photo 50. Bring the working needle back up through the fabric between the two beads where you want to tack down the next bead strand thread. See Photo 51.

Photo 49

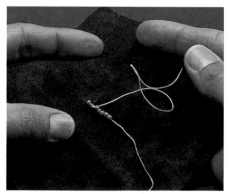

Photo 50

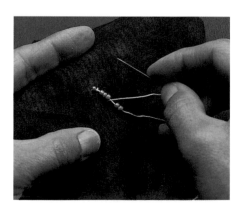

Photo 51

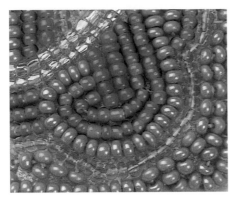
Couching

■ Needlepoint

To needlepoint with beads is very simple. Pick a needlepoint canvas size that will go with your bead size.

You can needlepoint with virtually any type of thread: beading thread, cotton crochet thread, embroidery floss, or whatever suits your project and beads.

The stitches for the project in this book go up and down, but they could just as easily go diagonally.

Make a basic sewing knot on the end of the thread. PNUT a hole of the needlepoint canvas. String a bead. PNDT hole, skipping one hole directly below the hole you just PNUT. See Photo 52. PNUT the hole that is diagonally across the hole you PNUT. See Photo 53. String a bead. PNDT hole,

skipping one hole directly below the hole you just PNUT. Repeat using different color beads according to the design chart. If the canvas doesn't fit the beads, or the beads look crowded, adjust by skipping a hole or two every stitch. When finished with one color (if you are matching the color of thread to the color of bead), or if you run out of thread, tie a sewing knot on the underside of the piece.

Miscellaneous Techniques

■ Knots

Knowing different knots can really come in handy when doing bead work. Some of them are the overhand knot, the surgeon's knot, and the double half-hitch knot (also known as the clove-hitch knot).

To tie an overhand knot, take the left end of the thread, pass it over and then under the right end. See Fig. 13. Pull tight.

The surgeon's knot used in this book is a variation of the one used by doctors. To tie a the knot, take the left end of the thread and pass it over, under, over, and under the

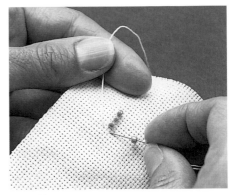
Photo 52

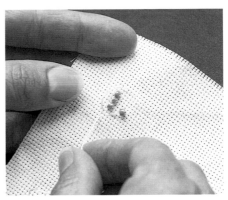
Photo 53

Figure 13

Bead needlepoint with size 11° seed beads

Bead needlepoint with Delica beads

Figure 14

Figure 15

right end. Next, take the right end, and pass it over, under, over, and under the left end. See Fig. 14. Pull tight.

To tie the clove-hitch knot, bring the working thread under and over the stationary thread, then under and over the stationary thread again, and through the loop formed by the working thread. See Fig. 15. Pull tight.

■ Anchor Thread or Weave-in End

These terms are used often in the projects in this book. As knots aren't used in many of the stitches, secure the thread by weaving it into the body of the piece. You can lock your ending thread in place by passing the needle through a nearby thread. Then weave in a zigzag pattern through the beads until it is hidden and secured. Cut off tail.

To start a new thread in the middle of a project, follow the same principle as weaving in the end, except in reverse. Weave the thread in a zigzag pattern through the beads until it is coming out of the bead that you left off on. Then start beading again.

■ Blocking

After you knit, crochet, or needle-point a piece, it is sometimes necessary to block it in order to set (and sometimes adjust) the stitches. This will ensure that the piece is square and the edges lie flat. This often improves the look of a finished item by eliminating any unevenness. An easy way to do this is in your home oven. Turn the oven on to 200°. Wet the needlework in cool water until the thread is soaked throughout. Blot out the excess water with a dish towel and then place the needlework right-side up on a cookie sheet. Adjust the rows of stitches, beads, and selvedge edges so that they are flat and line up vertically and horizontally. Place the cookie sheet in the oven and turn off the oven. Leave in the oven for several hours, or overnight, until the piece is dry.

3

BEAD WEAVING: NEEDLE AND LOOM PROJECTS

Sea Horse Journal

Jane Davis

The transparent quality of the beads in this piece is accentuated as you open your journal to make an entry and watch the sea horse illuminated from behind. The ocean background can be completed either by following the design chart bead by bead, or by gradually changing the colors without a chart (as was done in the sample).

The journal measures 6½" x 6" and the beadwork measures 2" x 2½".

MATERIALS

½ gram Japanese tubular beads, dyed matte transparent dark amber, Delica #777 (for sea horse)

1 gram Japanese tubular beads, dyed matte transparent amber, Delica #781 (for sea horse)

½ gram Japanese tubular beads, matte cantaloupe, Delica #852 (for sea horse)

½ gram Japanese tubular beads, transparent dark tangerine, Delica #704 (for sea horse)

2½ grams Japanese tubular beads, lined green/lime, Delica #274 (for background)

2½ grams Japanese tubular beads, emerald gold luster, Delica #125 (for background)

2½ grams Japanese tubular beads, lined green/teal luster, Delica #275 (for background)

2½ grams Japanese tubular beads, silver-lined teal, Delica #607 (for background)

2½ grams Japanese tubular beads, lined crystal/green aqua luster, Delica #238 (for background)

2½ grams Japanese tubular beads, lined blue AB, Delica #77 (for background)

2½ grams Japanese tubular beads, semi-matte silver-lined medium blue, Delica #693 (for background)

2½ grams Japanese tubular beads, luster cobalt, Delica #277 (for background)

White beading thread size B

Beading needle size 10

Journal

Exacto knife

Cutting surface

Metal ruler

Suede leather scraps

1¾" x 2¼" clear rigid plastic or Plexiglas™

Thick white glue or leather glue

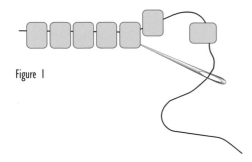

Figure 1

Glue

Figure 2

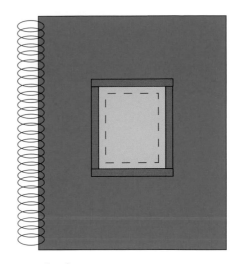

Figure 3

ROWS 1–2: String forty lined green/lime beads.

ROW 3: String one lined green/lime bead, skip the last bead from the previous row, and PNBT the next bead. See Fig. 1. Repeat across the row using all lined green/lime beads.

ROWS 4–76: Continue in peyote stitch, back and forth, following the design chart. Weave in ends.

With an Exacto knife and ruler, cut a 1³/₄" x 2¹/₄" hole in the center of the book cover. Cut a piece of plastic, or Plexiglas, to fit the hole and glue it edge to edge in the hole, flush with the front of the cover. Center the beaded piece on the front of the cover over the plastic and, using thick white glue, secure it in place along the edges where the beads extend onto the cover. See Fig. 2.

Cut a leather frame 3" x 3¹/₂" with a 1¹/₂" x 2¹/₄" window (the sides of the leather will be about ⁵/₈" wide). Cut two strips of leather ¹/₄" x 3¹/₂" and two strips of leather ¹/₄" x 2¹/₂". Glue the longer ¹/₄"-wide strips of leather along the beading and the shorter ¹/₄" strips above and below it. See Fig. 3. Glue the frame over the leather strips and the beading. Carefully line up the edges of the leather so they are flush.

- Dyed matte transparent dark amber, Delica #777
- Dyed matte transparent amber, Delica #781
- Matte cantaloupe, Delica #852
- Transparent dark tangerine, Delica #704
- Lined green/lime, Delica #274
- Emerald gold luster, Delica #125
- Lined green/teal luster, Delica #275
- Silver-lined teal, Delica #607
- Lined crystal/green aqua luster, Delica #238
- Lined blue AB, Delica #77
- Semi-matte silver-lined medium blue, Delica #693
- Luster cobalt, Delica #277

Dainty Violets Teacup and Saucer

Elizabeth Gourley

Spot of tea, anyone? Get your pinkies ready! This tiny teacup will make you feel quite grand. The Japanese cylinder beads used to make this teacup give it the look of fine bone china. It's a marvelous addition to anyone's teacup collection.

The finished cup measures 1" high and 3/4" wide. The saucer is 1 3/8" in diameter.

MATERIALS

White nylon beading thread size D
Beading needle size 11 or 12
Scissors
Sixteen Japanese tubular beads, silver-lined violet, Delica #610
Nine Japanese tubular beads, lined lime green, Delica #274
Four Japanese tubular beads, lavender, Delica #73
One Japanese tubular bead, opaque yellow, Delica #721
4 grams Japanese tubular beads, lined gold, Delica #042
7 grams Japanese tubular beads, Ceylon light yellow (off-white), Delica #203

■ Cup

ROUND 1: Using doubled thread so that cup will be stiff, string fifty gold beads. Do not make a knot. Weave in the ends later. PNBT all fifty beads to form a ring.

ROUND 2: This round is done with Ceylon light yellow beads (off-white) in the tubular double drop pcyotc stitch. String two beads. Skip next two gold beads from Round 1. PNT next two gold beads. See Fig. 1. Repeat this stitch all the way around ring. Make sure ring of beads stays tight.

ROUND 3: Same as Round 2. Keep beads tight and make sure they go down, and not out, from the ring.

ROUND 4: PNT the first two beads from Round 3. String two beads, skip two beads, and PNT next two beads. By Round 4, you will know which two beads to PNT because they will be the ones from the round beneath and they will be sticking up higher than the two beads you skipped from two rounds before. On every other round at the beginning of the round, you must PNT the first two beads from the round below before stringing the two beads.

ROUND 5: Same as Round 3, except start colored beads according to the design chart. The colored beads can be started just about anywhere on this round.

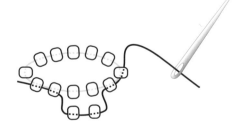

Figure 1

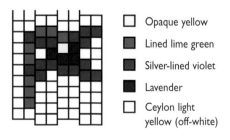

☐ Opaque yellow
◩ Lined lime green
■ Silver-lined violet
■ Lavender
☐ Ceylon light yellow (off-white)

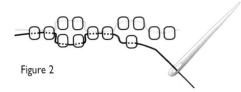

Figure 2

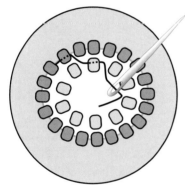

Detail of Dainty Violets Teacup and Saucer

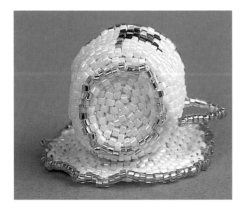

Figure 3

Figure 4

Keep working in the double drop peyote stitch, adding colored beads as shown on design chart, until Round 21.

ROUND 21: Decrease one bead every third stitch for a total of three decreases. Decrease by stringing one bead instead of two. See Fig. 2.

ROUND 22: Do not decrease. Work in double drop peyote.

ROUND 23: String one bead in the three decreases from ROUND 21 and decrease three more times in between the three other decrease stitches.

ROUND 24: Same as ROUND 22.

ROUND 25: String one bead for every one stitch instead of two (peyote stitch).

ROUNDS 26–28: Same as Round 25.

ROUND 29: This round starts the foot of the cup. String two gold beads for every stitch (double drop peyote).

ROUND 30: String one gold bead for every stitch (peyote stitch). When you are finished with the round, PNT the gold beads of both Round 29 and 30. This will form one stiff, straight round of gold beads.

ROUND 31: This round starts filling up the bottom of the cup. You must work with the cup upside down. PNT until thread is coming out of one of the Ceylon light yellow beads (off-white) along bottom edge. See Fig. 3. String one bead for each stitch (peyote stitch). This round is hard and awkward.

ROUNDS 32–33: Same as 31, but not as hard and awkward.

ROUND 34: Decrease every other stitch. For the decreases on this round, do not string a bead, just PNT.

ROUND 35: Do not decrease. There will only be one or two stitches left on this round. PNT last beads. Tighten thread and close up hole. Weave in end.

■ Handle

Using doubled thread, string eighteen gold beads. Skip last bead strung and PNBT all seventeen beads. Attach top of handle to cup by PNT the bead on the 6th round down from the top of the cup and five stitches (each stitch is a group of two beads) away from violet. Then PNBT the beads of the handle. Attach bottom of the handle to the bead on the 12th round directly below top of handle. Pull thread tight. Handle should bend into proper shape and be very stiff. Weave in end.

■ Saucer

The saucer is done in the flat circular peyote stitch. Be careful not to pull the thread too tight, and don't get discouraged. Sometimes the flat circular peyote stitch doesn't want to stay flat, especially after about the 5th round. Just keep at it and eventually you'll have a flat saucer. The saucer is done in the Ceylon light yellow (off-white) bead, except for the last two rounds.

ROUND 1: Use doubled thread about 3' long. String three beads. PNBT first bead strung and pull tight to make a circle.

ROUND 2: String two beads. PNT second bead of Round 1. String two beads. PNT next bead of Round 1. String two beads. PNT last bead of Round 1. See Fig. 4.

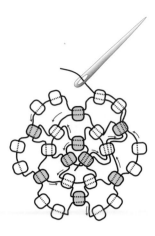

Figure 5

ROUND 3: PNT first bead of Round 2. String one bead and PNT the next bead. Repeat until the end of the round by putting one bead between every bead of Round 2 (total of six beads).

ROUND 4: String two beads. PNT next bead of Round 3. Repeat until end of round. There will be two beads between each bead of Round 3 (total of twelve beads). See Fig. 5.

ROUND 5: PNT first two beads of Round 4. *String one bead. PNT next two beads of Round 4*. Repeat between asterisks until end of round (total of six beads). On every other round you will have to PNT first bead or beads of previous round before you begin round.

ROUND 6: String two beads. PNT next bead of previous round. Repeat until end of round.

ROUND 7: PNT first two beads of previous round. *String one bead. PNT next two beads.* Repeat between asterisks until end of round.

ROUND 8: *String one bead. PNT next bead of previous round. String two beads. PNT next bead of previous round.* Repeat between asterisks until the end of round.

ROUND 9: Same as Round 7.

ROUND 10: Same as Round 6.

ROUND 11: Same as Round 7.

ROUND 12: *String one bead. PNT next bead or beads of previous round.* Repeat between asterisks until end of round.

ROUND 13: Same as Round 12.

ROUND 14: Same as Round 8.

ROUND 15: Same as Round 12.

ROUND 16: *String two gold beads. PNT next bead of previous round.* Repeat between asterisks until end of round.

ROUND 17: PNT first two beads of Round 16. *String one gold bead. PNT next two beads of previous round.* Repeat between asterisks until end of round.

ROUND 18: PNBT rounds 16 and 17 all at once to create one round of gold beads. Weave in end.

Needle Case Pendant

Jane Davis

This pendant, with its long twisted fringe and antique drop beads, is also useful as a needle case. The body of the case is constructed in circular peyote stitch while the lid begins increasing from three beads in circular peyote and continues down the side of the lid in one/two drop peyote. This is a good project for learning even-count circular peyote stitch and increases in peyote stitch. The finished needle case is an elegant addition to your sewing supplies, or you can embellish it with the chain and fringe as shown in the photo.

The finished pendant and fringe measure 5³/₄" on a 27¹/₂" chain.

MATERIALS

FOR NEEDLE CASE

Wooden needle case, painted and varnished at opening

5 grams Japanese tubular beads, opaque alabaster luster, Delica #211 (for background)

¹/₂ gram Japanese tubular beads, matte metallic sea-foam green, Delica #374 (for leaves)

¹/₂ gram Japanese tubular beads, matte metallic teal iris, Delica #327 (for leaves)

¹/₂ gram Japanese tubular beads, matte lavender, Delica #356 (for flowers)

¹/₂ gram Japanese tubular beads, sparkling purple-lined crystal, Delica #906 (for flowers)

¹/₂ gram Japanese tubular beads, silver-lined wine, Delica #611 (for flowers)

Twenty-two Japanese tubular beads, matte opaque sky blue, Delica #879 (for ribbon)

Twelve Japanese tubular beads, matte opaque light blue, Delica #881 (for ribbon)

FOR FRINGE AND NECK CHAIN

¹/₄ oz or 5 grams transparent purple seed beads, size 15°

¹/₄ oz or 7 grams matte purple seed beads, size 11°

¹/₈ oz or 2¹/₂ grams burgundy/purple seed beads, size 8°

Eighteen ¹/₂" matte lavender bugle beads

Thirty-two ¹/₂"-deep purple bugle beads

Thirty 4mm round beads, light green

Ten bi-cone beads, light green

Six cylinder ¹/₄"-long beads, light green

Two flower drops, purple

Three 13mm oval Czech "Satin" beads, purple with pink flowers

Four oval faceted beads, purple

Eight transparent center drilled disks, purple

Thirteen transparent center drilled flower disks, purple

Thirty 4mm Swarovski crystals, purple

Eighteen side drilled drops, purple

Two silver end cap beads

Two silver spacers

One silver bead

Size 10 and 13 beading needles

Beading thread, size B for case, 00 for neck chain, and size 0 for fringe

- ▢ Alabaster luster, #211
- ▨ Matte lavender, #356
- ■ Sparkling purple-lined crystal, #906
- ■ Silver-ined wine, #611
- ▨ Matte metallic sea-foam green, #374
- ▨ Matte metallic teal iris, #327
- ▨ Matte opaque sky blue, #879
- ▨ Matte opaque light blue, #881
- ▢ First bead in round
- ▲ Start fringe here
- ✳ Attach neck chain here

Design Chart 1

■ Needle Case Body

ROUNDS 1–2: String thirty-six cream beads and tie them tightly into a circle with a square knot around the wooden needle case body.

ROUND 3: String one cream bead, skip a bead, and PNT the next bead on the ring of beads. Repeat around the needle case. PNT the first bead in Round 3 again.

ROUNDS 4–53: Continue in peyote stitch, following the Design Chart 1 pattern. Round 50 should be at the bottom edge of the needle case. If it is too short or long, add or unstring enough rounds so the beading just covers the needle case and is ready for decreasing. Adjust the triangle, indicating where to begin the fringe on Design Chart 1, if necessary.

■ Bottom of Needle Case

ROUND 54: String one bead and PNT two beads of previous row. Repeat for round. PNT first bead in round.

ROUND 55: String two beads and PNT next bead on previous round. Repeat for round. PNT first two beads in round.

ROUND 56: String one bead and PNT the next two beads in previous round. Repeat around. PNT first bead in round.

ROUND 57: String one bead and PNT the next bead in previous round. Repeat around. PNT first bead in round.

ROUND 58: String one bead and PNT the next two beads in previous round. Repeat twice more. String one bead and PNT the next three beads in previous round. PNT first bead in round.

ROUND 59: String one bead and PNT the next bead in previous round. Repeat three more times. PNT these last four beads again, knot, and weave in end.

■ Needle Case Lid

ROUND 1: Begin the needle case lid by stringing one of each of the three colors of purple beads. Tie into a circle with a square knot. See Fig. 1.

Figure 1

ROUND 2: String two light purple beads and PNT the next bead in Round 1. Repeat twice more. PNT the first bead in Round 2.

ROUND 3: String one cream bead and PNT the next bead in Round 2. Continue in this manner, following the color sequence in Design Chart 2. PNT the first bead in Round 3.

ROUND 4: String one cream and one dark green bead and PNT the next bead in Round 3. Continue around, following the color sequence in Design Chart 2. PNT the first bead in Round 4.

ROUND 5: String one cream bead and PNT the next bead in Round 4. Repeat around, following the color sequence in Design Chart 2. PNT the first bead in Round 5.

ROUND 6: String one dark green bead and PNT the next bead in Round 5. Repeat around, following the color sequence in Design Chart 2. PNT the first bead in Round 6.

ROUND 7: Following the color sequence in Design Chart 2, string two beads and PNT the next bead in Round 6. Repeat around. This is both

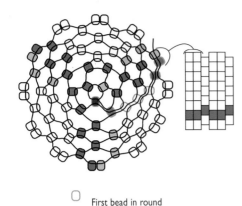

○　First bead in round

Design Chart 2

the last round in the circular design chart and the top round in the flat design chart of Design Chart 2. Now place your beading on the top of the wooden needle case lid and continue beading.

ROUNDS 8–17: Repeat Round 6 and Round 7 alternately in cream beads.

ROUNDS 18–19: Repeat Round 6 and Round 7 in dark green beads.

ROUNDS 20–21: Repeat Round 6 and Round 7 in cream beads. The beads should extend one bead-width beyond the wooden lid. If the beading is too short or too long, add or unstring enough rounds so the beading just covers the lid. Tie off the thread and weave in the end.

Glue the finished lid to the wooden needle case lid. The last row of beads will just pass the edge of the wooden lid.

■ Neck Chain

Take a 9' length of size 00 beading thread. Double it and weave it into needle case body so that it comes out of the left side of the right top starred bead on Design Chart 1. String three size 15° beads, one cylinder, three size 15° beads. PNT

the left side of the right bottom starred bead on Design Chart 1 and through three or four more beads away. See Fig. 2. PNBT several beads on the body of the needle case to help distribute the weight of the neck chain over more beads than just the starred beads. Finish with the thread coming out of the right side of the right bottom starred bead.

String two size 15° beads. PNT one size 15° bead, the cylinder bead, and one size 15° bead. See Fig. 3.

String two size 15° beads and PNT the right top starred bead right to left. Repeat the process of passing the needle through several beads on the body of the needle case for strength. Finish by coming out of the left side of the right top starred bead. PNBT the first three size 15° beads, the cylinder, and one size 15° bead below the cylinder.

String twenty-five size 15° beads, one size 11° bead, one oval diamond bead, and one size 11° bead. PNBT the oval diamond and size 11° bead. String twenty-five size 15° beads and then, holding the thread close to the strung beads, roll the thread in one direction between your fingers until it kinks (about ten to fifteen times). Be careful not to release the thread or the twist will unwind. PNBT the bottom size 15° bead, the cylinder bead, and the top size 15° bead. Don't let go of the twisted thread until you have pulled it almost all the way through these beads. Adjust the twisted strands of beads so that they spiral evenly.

String the neck chain according to Fig. 4. String one size 15° bead, one cylinder, and one size 15° bead. Make a twisted dangle like the one at the beginning of the other end of the neck chain by PNBT one size 15° bead, the cylinder, and one size 15° bead after twisting the beading thread between your fingers. String

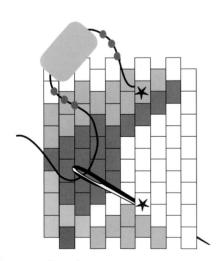

Figure 2

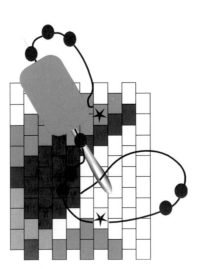

Figure 3

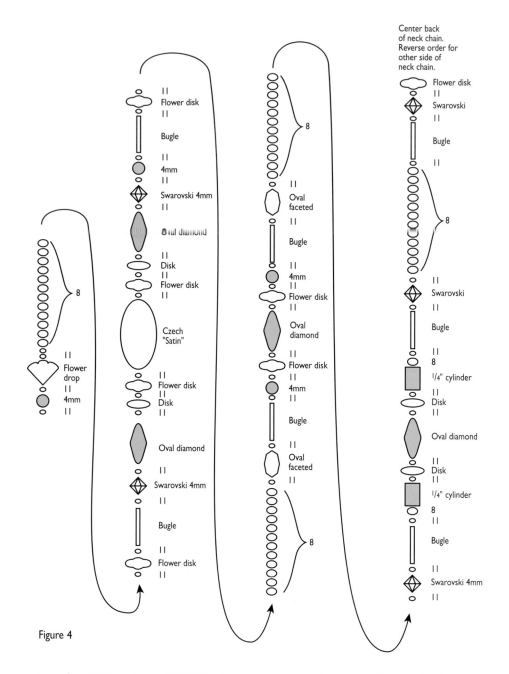

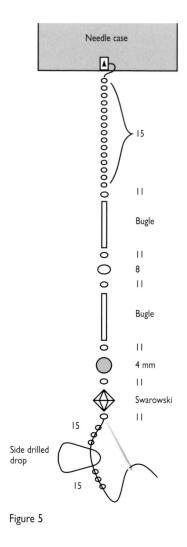

Figure 4

Figure 5

two size 15° beads and PNT the top starred bead on the left side of the needle case. PNBT several beads on the body of the needle case to help distribute the weight of the neck chain over more beads than just the starred beads. Finish with the thread coming out of the opposite side of the top starred bead on the left side of the needle case. String two size 15° beads and PNT the size 15° bead, the cylinder bead, and the next size 15° bead. String two size 15° beads and PNT the bottom left starred bead on the needle case. Repeat the above

steps of passing the needle through the beads on the case to strengthen it. String two beads and PNBT the size 15° bead, the cylinder, and three size 15° beads to the needle case. Weave in end.

■ Fringe

Begin with a 6' length of size 0 beading thread coming out the right side of the starting fringe bead, as indicated with the triangle on Design Chart 1.

String fifteen size 15° beads, one size 11° bead, one dark purple bugle bead, one size 11° bead. one size 8° bead, one size 11° bead, one light purple bugle bead, one size 11° bead, one 4mm round bead, one size 11° bead, one Swarovski bead, one size 11° bead, three size 15° beads, one drop bead, and three size 15° beads.

Skip the last seven beads and PNBT all the other beads except the first fifteen size 15° beads. See Fig. 5.

String fifteen size 15° beads and twist the strand as for the twisted dangle on the neck chain. See Fig. 6.

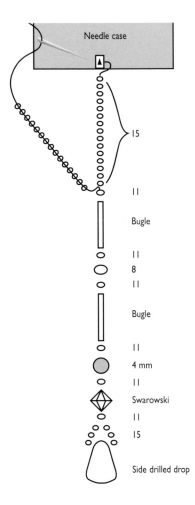

Needle case

}15

| | Bugle

| | 8

| | Bugle

| | 4 mm

| | Swarowski

| | 15

Side drilled drop

Figure 6

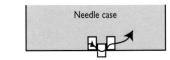

Needle case

Figure 7

PNT the starting fringe bead from left to right and through one more bead diagonally below. PNT the next bead diagonally above. See Fig. 7.

The first strand of fringe is complete. You are ready to make the next. Continue in the same manner by making one twisted strand of the fringe in each Delica bead around the needle case and increasing the twisted size 15° beads by five beads in each strand until there are nine finished strands and fifty-five size 15° beads in each half of the last made twist.

Repeat the last made strand (fifty-five size 15° beads) and then decrease by five size 15° beads in each twist. Finish with the last twist having fifteen size 15° beads, which is next to the first strand that has fifteen size 15° beads. Weave in end.

■ Dangle in Center Bottom of Needle Case Pendant

Begin with a 6-foot length of size 0 beading thread coming out one of the Delica beads on the bottom of the case in the 4th to the last round.

String seven size 15° beads, one size 11° bead, one size 8° bead, one size 11° bead, one swarovski crystal, one size 11° bead, one 4mm round bead, one size 11° bead, one silver spacer, one size 11° bead, one silver end cap, one Czech "Satin" bead, one silver end cap, one size 11° bead, one silver spacer, one size 11° bead, one 4mm round, one size 11° bead, one silver bead, one size 11° bead, one swarovski crystal, one size 11° bead, and twenty-one size 15° beads. See Fig. 8.

Skip the twenty-one size 15° beads and PNBT all the other beads except the first six size 15° beads.

String six size 15° beads and PNT one Delica on the opposite side of the case bottom from the first size 15° bead.

PNT several Delicas until the thread is coming out a Delica about ⅓ of the way away. String six size 15° beads and PNBT all the beads on the strand except the last size 15° beads.

String ten size 15° beads, PNT the 11th bead on the size 15° bead loop. String ten size 15° beads and PNBT the strand coming out the first size 15° bead at the top.

String six size 15° beads and PNT one Delica opposite from the

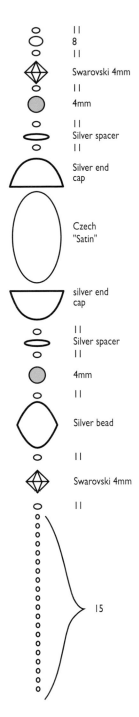

| | 8

○○ | |

◇ Swarovski 4mm

| | 4mm

○ Silver spacer

| | Silver end cap

Czech "Satin"

silver end cap

| | Silver spacer

| | 4mm

| | Silver bead

| | Swarovski 4mm

| | 15

Figure 8

previous six size 15° beads. PNT several Delicas until the thread is coming out a Delica between two size 15° bead strands.

String six size 15° beads, and PNT one or two of the threads where the other strands enter the size 15° bead at the top of the dangle. Tie a slip knot. String six size 15° beads and PNT a Delica opposite. Weave in end.

Monogrammed Scissors Case with Needle Book

Jane Davis

This is the perfect case for your favorite pair of scissors as well as a monogrammed needle book so everyone will know that it is yours. The floral design is the same as the Needle Case Pendant project (see p. 35), so you can make a matching set. The uneven peyote stitch in large size 8° beads leads to intricate finishing details, which give this project its elegant detail.

The finished piece measures 2³/4" x 4¹/2" when closed. Fits 3³/4" stork scissors.

MATERIALS

FOR MONOGRAMMED NEEDLE BOOK
4 grams Japanese tubular beads, opaque alabaster luster, Delica #211 (for background)
¹/2 gram Japanese tubular beads, matte metallic sea-foam green, Delica #374 (for leaves)
¹/2 gram Japanese tubular beads, matte metallic teal iris, Delica #327 (for leaves)
1 gram Japanese tubular beads, matte lavender, Delica #356 (for flowers)
¹/2 gram Japanese tubular beads, sparkling purple-lined crystal, Delica #906 (for flowers)
¹/2 gram Japanese tubular beads, silver lined wine, Delica #611 (for flowers)
Twenty-two Japanese tubular beads, dyed opaque squash, Delica #651 (for ribbon)
Twelve Japanese tubular beads, lined topaz/yellow AB, Delica #272 (for ribbon)
5 grams light purple size 15° seed beads
Suede leather scrap or ultra suede
Scrap of felt or felted wool
Beading thread size B white
Snap

FOR SCISSORS CASE
1¹/2 oz or 41 grams metallic burgundy size 8° seed beads
¹/4 oz or 5 grams metallic burgundy size 15° seed beads
¹/2 gram Japanese tubular beads, matte light amethyst AB, Delica #857
¹/2 gram Japanese tubular beads, transparent raspberry, Delica #104
Beading thread size F and O to match color of size 8° seed beads
Large oval bead for closure
1 yd ¹/8" wide ribbon for sides of scissors case
Suede leather scraps or ultra suede for lining

Beading needles size 10 and 13
Scissors

■ Scissors Case Needle Book Side and Flap with Large Oval Bead Closure

Follow Design Chart 1 and the instructions below to complete the needle book side and flap of the scissors case with size 8° seed beads.

ROWS 1–3: Using a 12' length of size F beading thread and size 8° beads, string thirty-one beads, leaving a 3' tail to be used to complete the flap in the opposite direction. String one bead, PNBT the 30th bead, and pull the beads tight. String one bead, skip the next bead, and PNT the next bead. Pull tight. Repeat across the

row until the last bead. String one bead and PNT the last bead towards the finished beading. See Fig. 1. Weave through the beads to position the thread for the first bead in Row 4. See Fig. 2.

ROW 4: String one bead, skip a bead, and PNT the next bead. Repeat across the row.

ROW 5: String one bead, skip a bead, and PNT the next bead. Repeat across the row until the last bead. String one bead, PNT the end bead of Row 3 towards the finished beading, and weave through the beads to position the thread for the first bead in the next row. See Fig. 3.

ROWS 6–19: Continue as in Rows 4 and 5.

ROW 20: Continue across as in Row 4. At the end, weave through the beads to position the thread for a decrease row. See Fig. 4.

ROW 21: String one bead, skip a bead, PNT the next bead. Repeat across the row.

ROW 22: Same as Row 5.

ROW 23. Same as Row 4.

ROW 24: Same as Row 5.

ROWS 25–79: Repeat the sequence of

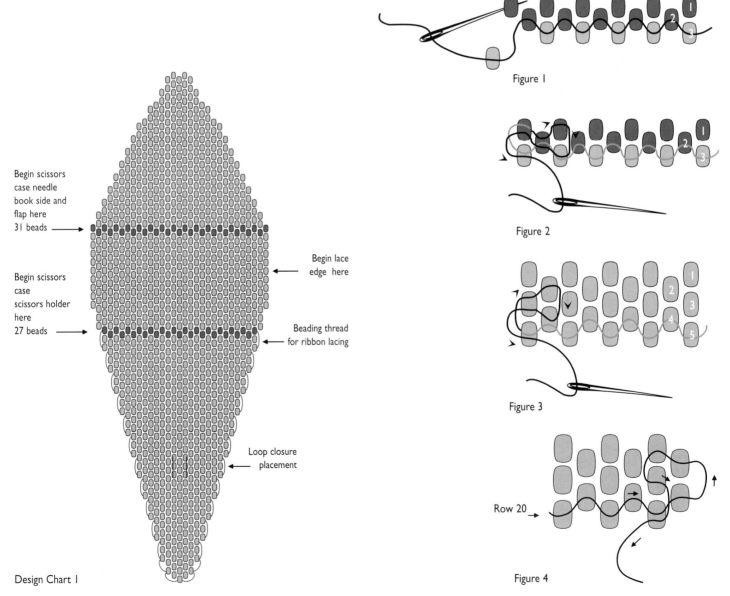

Begin scissors case needle book side and flap here
31 beads

Begin scissors case scissors holder here
27 beads

Begin lace edge here

Beading thread for ribbon lacing

Loop closure placement

Design Chart 1

Figure 1

Figure 2

Figure 3

Row 20

Figure 4

thread, follow the steps in Fig. 6 and Fig. 7 for the closure at the end of the flap. Repeat Steps 4 through 7 until there are thirteen rows of Delicas. Then complete Step 8 by stringing the number of Delicas needed for the size bead used. PNT the beads in Step 8 twice to strengthen it. Weave in ends.

■ Scissors Case Scissors Holder Side with Delica Loop for Closure

ROWS 1–4: Stitch the same as the front, starting with twenty-seven beads.

ROW 5: Same as Row 19 on scissors case front.

ROWS 6–60: Repeat the sequence of Rows 20–24, as for the scissors case front, ten times. There will be four beads in the last row completed. Repeat Rows 80–83, as for the scissors case front, strengthen the "V," and make the side loops for the 1/8" ribbon, as for the scissors case front.

Make a three-bead-wide loop of peyote stitch with Delica beads or sizes 8° seed beads (using Fig. 6 and Fig. 7 left as a guide). The loop needs to be just big enough for the large oval bead to slip through on the back of the scissors case. Anchor to the scissors case where indicated on Design Chart 1. To strengthen the closure area, stitch through the front suede lining several times, anchoring the loop to the lining. Knot and weave in end.

■ Lace Edging Along Flap

To make the lace edging of loops of beads and picots along the flap, adhere a 9' length of thread so that it is coming out the size 8 bead on the right side where indicated on Design

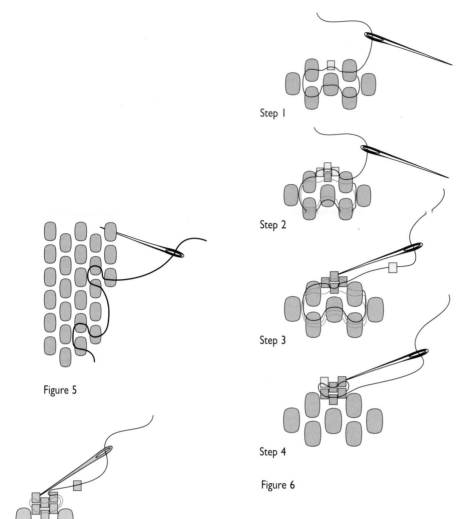

Step 1

Step 2

Step 3

Step 4

Figure 6

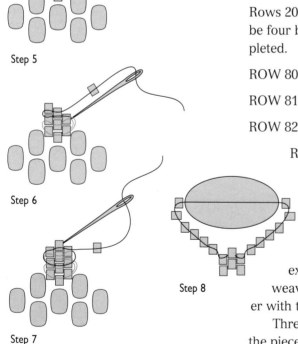

Figure 5

Step 5

Step 6

Step 7

Figure 7

Step 8

Rows 20–24 eleven times. There will be four beads in the last row completed.

ROW 80: Repeat Row 4

ROW 81: Repeat Row 20.

ROW 82: Repeat Row 20.

ROW 83: Repeat Row 20.

PNT the bottom "V" of the beads to reinforce the edge. Make a loop of thread along each edge up to Row 25. See Fig. 5. This extra stitch will be used to weave the front and back together with the 1/8" wide ribbon.

Thread the 3' tail at the top of the piece and stitch in the opposite direction, repeating Rows 20, 4, and 5 eight times. Using size O beading

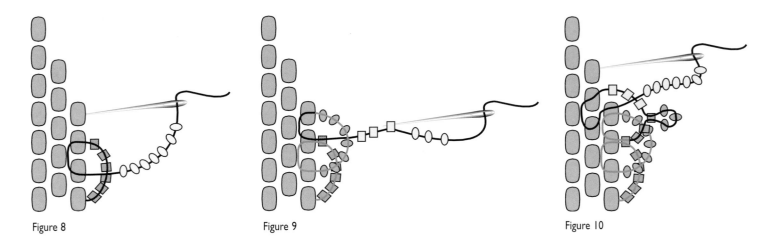

Figure 8

Figure 9

Figure 10

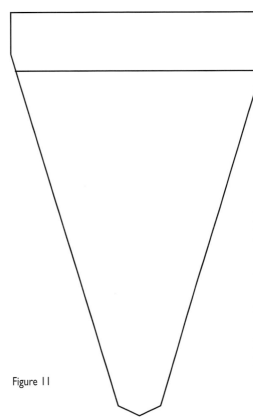

Figure 11

Detail of Monogrammed Scissors Case with Needle Book

Chart 1. String six matte light amethyst AB beads, Delica #857. Working towards the tip of the flap, along the size 8 beads at the edge of the piece, skip a bead and PNT the next bead, then PNT the skipped bead. Making each new loop of beads in front of the previous loop, string seven size 15 light purple seed beads, skip a bead, PNT the next bead. See Fig. 8 for the sequence. PNT the bead skipped and through one Delica. String five matte lavender beads, Delica #356. Skip a bead on the edge of the piece and PNT the next bead. PNT the bead skipped. String seven of the seed beads, skip a bead, PNT the next bead, PNT the bead skipped and one Delica.

Now, following the same pattern of alternating Delicas and seed beads, begin making picots in each Delica loop. To do this, string three Delicas and three seed beads. PNBT the third Delica strung. String two Delicas, skip a bead on the side of the piece, PNT the next bead. As you stitch along the edge of the piece, you will now have to PNT two beads on every other stitch to have the thread come out of the bead skipped along the edge. See Figs. 9 and 10 for this sequence.

Continue in this pattern to the tip of the flap, then mirror the pattern on the other edge of the flap, always passing behind each previous loop rather than in front. Weave in ends.

■ **Scissors Case Construction**

Adjust Fig. 11, if necessary, so that it matches your finished beading. Then cut the front and back suede pieces from Fig. 11. Stitch together at the side seams with a running stitch about ⅛" from the edge of the suede. Stitch back the opposite way, filling in the open spaces of the first running stitch as you stitch in running stitch again. See Fig. 12. Stitch the edging of size 15° seed beads on the top of the front edge of the size 8° seed beads by following the steps in

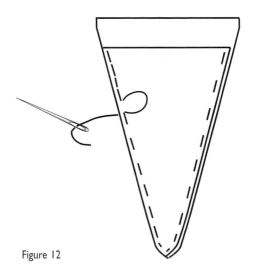

Figure 12

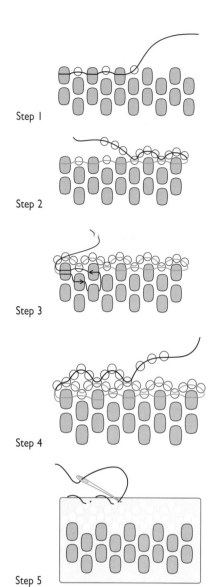

Step 1

Step 2

Step 3

Step 4

Step 5

Figure 13

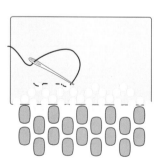

Figure 14

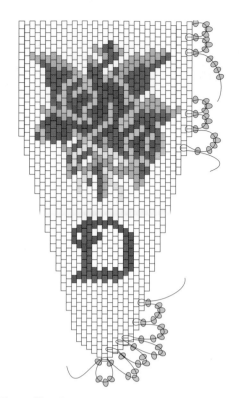

Design Chart 2

Detail of Monogrammed Scissors Case with Needle Book

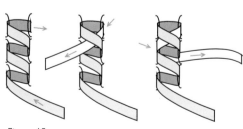

Figure 15

Fig. 13. Then stitch to the top edge of the suede. Stitch the back top suede edge to the size 8° seed beads, passing through a bead, then taking a stitch through the suede all across the edge. Repeat the pattern of size 15° seed beads, as on the front edge in Fig. 13, covering the overcast stitches and stitching down to the suede as in Fig. 14.

Starting at the bottom point of the case, weave the 1/8" ribbon along the case edge, up one side and then back down. See Fig. 15. Pass the bottom point and weave up the other side and back down to the bottom point again. Tie the two ends in a knot or hide in the weaving. Make a small tassel through the knot or the bottom point of the weaving.

■ The Needle Book

Following Design Chart 2, begin the needle book cover using peyote stitch with Delica beads and size B beading thread through Row 44. Beginning at Row 45, choose a monogram from Design Chart 3, and finish the needle book cover from that chart.

Adjust Fig. 16, if necessary, so that it matches your finished beading. Then cut the suede backing for the needle book from Fig. 16 and attach the male side of the snap. Stitch it to the Delica beads, passing through one bead on the edge of the piece and then taking a small stitch through the suede all around the piece. Using size 15° seed beads, follow Design Chart 2 and make the edging along the sides and point of the needle case cover.

Cut the felt from Fig. 16 and stitch the female side of the snap to the felt. Then blind-hem it to the back of the scissors case, passing through a size 8° bead and then tak-

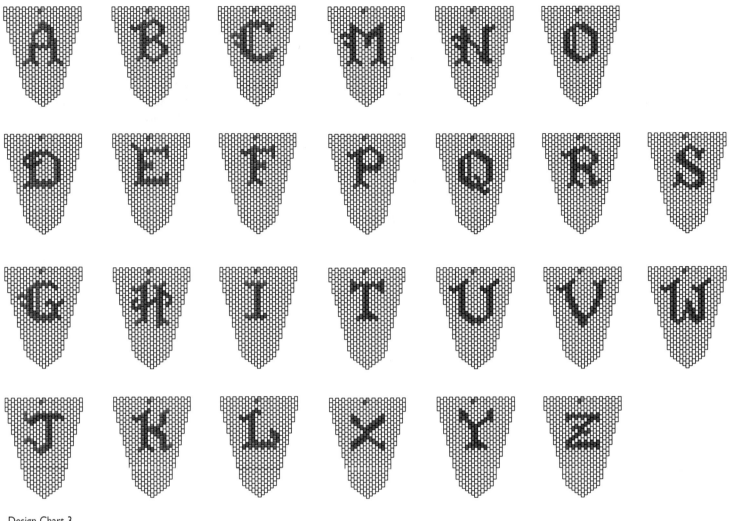

Design Chart 3

ing a stitch through the felt. Repeat all around the felt. Make sure the area around the snap is securely fastened to the scissors case, because this is a high-use area.

Stitch the needle cover to the felt at the top edge. Stitch the size 15° seed beads in a small picot inside the needle cover on the felt, covering your stitches that hold the cover to the felt. See Fig. 17.

Stitch an edging like Fig. 13 along the top of the needle cover and attach to the scissors case beads, covering the seam of suede and felt.

Figure 17

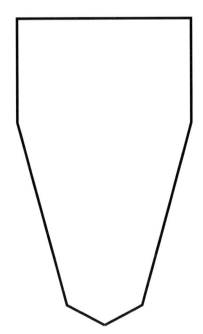

Figure 16

Detail of Monogrammed Scissors Case with Needle Book

Victorian Ivy Leaf Charm Bracelet

Elizabeth Gourley

The petite, sparkly charlotte beads used in this project take you back in time 100 years or so. I felt very Victorian as I made this delicate ivy leaf bracelet. The finished project has the look of a fragile antique.

The body of the bracelet is done in peyote stitch and the leaves are made with the square stitch, which lends itself well to making free forms. The finished measurements of the piece are 7" x 3/4".

MATERIALS

- 4 grams charlotte beads, navy blue
- 4 grams charlotte beads, translucent gray
- 2 grams charlotte beads, eggshell white
- 2 grams charlotte beads, translucent dark green
- 2 grams charlotte beads, translucent medium green
- 2 grams charlotte beads, light green
- One antique-style octagonal accent bead, cobalt blue
- White nylon beading thread, size 00
- Beading needle, size 15
- Scissors

■ Body of Bracelet

ROWS 1–3: Use about 6' of thread. String fourteen gray beads, leaving a tail about 1' long to use later for the end netting. String one gray bead. Skip the 14th gray bead strung. PNT next bead. *String one gray bead. Skip next gray bead. PNT next gray bead.* Repeat between asterisks until the last bead is passed through. Keep thread tension tight so the beads stack one upon the other. See Fig 1. This one row will form Rows 1–3. You will now have seven beads per row.

ROWS 4–7: Use gray beads. String one bead. PNT first bead that is extended farther up than the one next to it. *String one bead. PNT next bead from previous row (the first

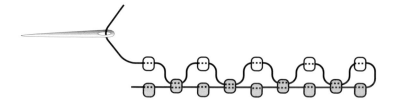

Figure 1

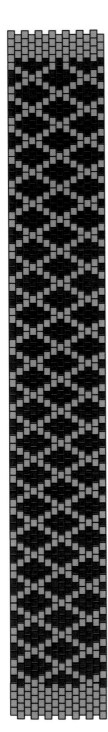

Design Chart 1

■ Navy blue
■ Translucent gray

bead sticking up farther than the other two around it).* Repeat between asterisks until the end of the row. Rows 5–7 are the same, using gray beads and the flat peyote stitch.

ROW 8: Work the same as the other rows, but you must start changing colors between the blue and gray beads according to Design Chart 1 to create the latticework look.

ROWS 9–165: Same as Row 8.

ROWS 166–172: Work in the peyote stitch using only gray beads.

■ End Netting

Working in netting stitch with gray beads, decrease one stitch on each end for five rows.

ROW 1: PNT first bead of previous row. String three beads. *PNT next bead. String three beads.* Repeat between asterisks three more times (total of five stitches). On last stitch, PNT last two beads of previous row. See Fig. 2.

ROW 2: PNT top bead of last netting stitch. *String three beads. PNT top bead of next netting stitch.* Repeat between asterisks three more times (total of four stitches).

ROW 3: Same as Row 2, except total of three stitches.

ROW 4: Make two netting stitches.

ROW 5: Make one netting stitch.

Weave in end or, if it's long enough, use for closure. Repeat Rows 1–5 on other end of the bracelet. End netting should look like Fig. 2.

■ Loop Closure

To form bracelet loop closure, work the thread so that it is coming out of the top bead of the end netting. String twenty-three gray beads. PNBT the top bead in the opposite direction of the thread that came out of it. See Fig. 3. Weave in end, making it secure.

To form large bead clasp on the other end of the bracelet, work the thread so that it is coming out of the top bead of end netting. String three gray beads, one octagonal accent bead, one gray bead. (Charlotte beads are so small that you have to pick your accent bead carefully so that the charlotte will not go through the accent bead hole.) PNBT accent bead and then the three gray beads. PNBT the top netting bead in the

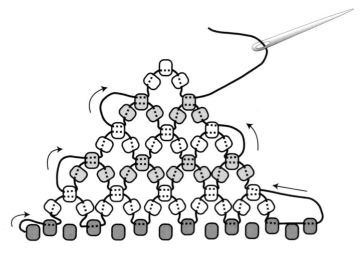

Figure 2

Figure 3

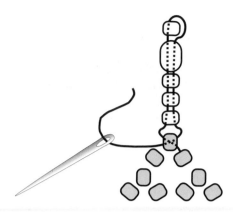

Figure 4

opposite direction of the thread that came out of it. See Fig. 4. Weave in end.

■ Side Edge Netting

Secure the thread so that it is coming out of the first bead of peyote stitch on the side edge of the bracelet. *String three gray beads. PNDT next bead of bracelet edge. PNUT the next bead.* Repeat between asterisks all along the edge of the bracelet. See Fig. 5. Repeat on other side edge.

■ Leaves

The leaves are done in the square stitch. All the leaves start the same way but vary in size and shape the way real leaves do. Vary the color of the leaves with all three greens, making sure that the darkest green goes in one line up the leaf for the vein.

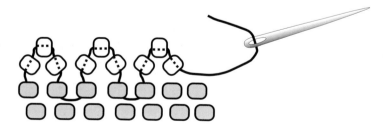

Figure 5

Use the white beads to outline the leaves. I made nine leaves, but you can add more, if desired.

ROWS 1–2: Start at the tip of the leaf by making a small white triangle. String two white beads (these will be the second row). String one white bead. PNT the first white bead strung in the opposite direction of the row. PNBT the third bead strung. See Fig. 6. PNT the two white beads on the second row. This will form the triangle.

ROW 3: This row is worked in the regular square stitch with increases of one bead on each side. String one white and one dark green bead. PNT (in the opposite direction as the row) first bead on second row. PNBT (in the same direction as the row) the green bead just strung on. String one green bead. PNT (in opposite direction) second bead on second row. PNBT (in same direction) green bead that was just strung on. String one white bead (this is the increased bead). Go on to the next row using last strung white bead as last bead in Row 3. The row ends with a total of four beads (two green in the middle and two white on ends).

ROWS 4–8: Work same as Row 3, increasing one bead at the beginning and end of the row. The increased beads are white to ensure that the leaves are outlined in white. The rest

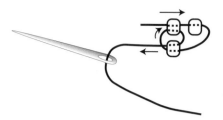

Figure 6

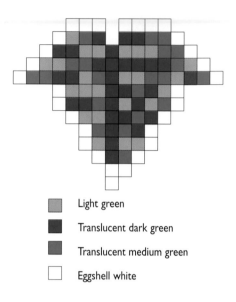

■ Light green

■ Translucent dark green

■ Translucent medium green

□ Eggshell white

Design Chart 2

of the row consists of random greens except for one dark green bead in the middle of the row (for the vein). See Design Chart 2 for guidance. On some leaves, don't increase every row so that you have some narrow leaves and some wide ones. For shorter and longer leaves, make six rows on some, eight rows on others before you go to the next step.

ROW 6 or 9: Depending on the leaf size, increase two to three beads at the beginning and end of the row. Keep white beads on the ends of the row and greens in the middle.

To increase more than one bead at the beginning of the row, string two or three beads, depending on

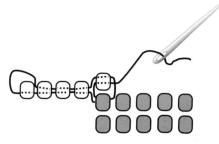

Figure 7

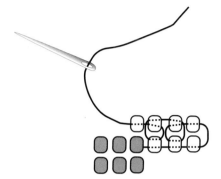

Figure 8

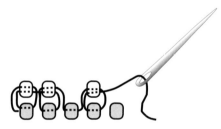

Figure 9

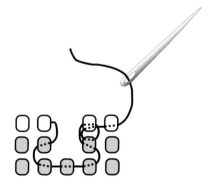

Figure 10

leaf size. Skip last bead strung and PNBT the other bead or beads strung. Then start row as normal. See Fig. 7.

It is easier to add beads on the end of the row. String two or three beads. Keep thread tension tight. Go to next row using strung beads as if they were part of row beneath. See Fig. 8.

ROW 7 or 10: Decrease one bead at the beginning and end of each row. Make sure the first and last beads are white.

To decrease one bead at the beginning of the row, simply PNBT second bead from the end and then begin your first stitch. To decrease at the end of the row, simply stop where the row ends.

Repeat Row 7 one or two more times, depending on size of leaf. On the second-to-last row (on most of the leaves this would be the third row after the large increase row), the middle bead (the dark green vein bead) is skipped to leave a space. See Fig. 9. This leaves room for the stem of the leaf.

The next row is the last row and all white beads are used. When you get to the space, PNT bead on row beneath and then through three beads directly below the space. PNT bead above the last of the three beads, bring thread up, and finish row. See Fig. 10.

■ Stem of Leaf

After the leaf is done, weave thread in so that it is coming out of the bead at the bottom of the space on top of the leaf. String from five to eight beads of random green colors. Skip last bead strung and PNBT all the other stem beads. See Fig. 11. Weave in end.

■ Vine

When all nine leaves are finished, they must be strung together on a vine. Start with 2' of thread. Use random green colors. String two beads. Leave a 6" tail to weave into body of bracelet later. PNT top bead of one leaf stem. String twenty-two beads. PNT top bead of next leaf stem. String one bead. PNT top bead of third leaf stem. String twelve beads. PNT top two beads of fourth leaf stem. String seventeen beads. PNT top two beads of fifth leaf stem. String twelve beads. PNT top bead of sixth leaf stem. String ten beads. PNT top two beads of seventh leaf stem. String fourteen beads. PNT top bead of eighth leaf's stem. String one green bead. PNT top bead of ninth leaf stem.

Once the vine is finished, attach it to the bracelet. Place the vine in a wavy line on the bracelet so that the leaves can fall in a natural way.

PNBT three beads of the vine. Attach to bracelet by PNT one bead of the bracelet. *PNT next five beads of vine and then attach to bracelet as before.* Make sure the vine lays flat. Repeat between the asterisks until the entire vine is attached. Weave in the end.

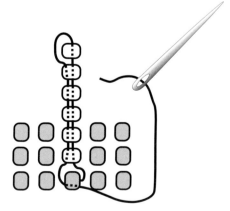

Figure 11

Beauty Is in the Eye of the Beholder: Peacock Amulet Bag Necklace

Elizabeth Gourley

The beautiful deep purple color of the beads used in this project makes the royal peacock seem even more royal. You'll feel majestic too with this amulet bag gracing your neck.

This project is done in the tubular brick stitch. The finished bag, not including the fringe, measures 2³/8" x 2³/4".

MATERIALS

20 grams Japanese tubular beads, silver-lined violet, Delica #610

10 grams Japanese tubular beads, semi-matte medium blue, Delica #693

7 grams Japanese tubular beads, lined lime green, Delica #274

7 grams Japanese tubular beads, dyed matte transparent Kelly green, Delica #776

5 grams Japanese tubular beads, silver-lined gold, Delica #042

4 grams Japanese tubular beads, lined topaz, Delica #065

One Japanese tubular bead black, Delica #010

Black nylon beading thread, size D

Two beading needles, size 11

Scissors

To begin the amulet bag, thread two needles on either end of a length of thread about 5' long. Make a ladder stitch row seventy-one blue beads long, as follows. String one bead. Move it to the middle of the thread. String one bead with one needle, then pass the other needle through the same bead. Make sure the needles pass in the opposite directions. Pull tight. See Fig. 1. Repeat using all seventy-one beads. Connect the first and last beads to make a ring. This

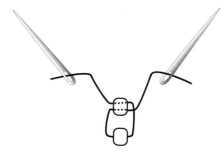

Figure 1

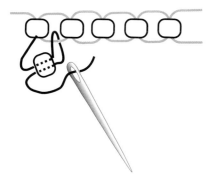

Figure 2

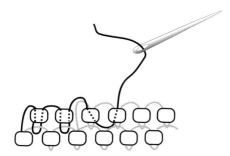

Figure 3

ring is the base from which you will build the body of the bag.

Use one needle to make the body of the bag and the other needle for the edging around the top. Work the bag from the top down by following the design chart from top to bottom. It doesn't matter where you place the design on the bag, because you can position the bag so that the design is in the center front when you sew up the bottom of the bag.

■ Body of Bag

ROUND 1: Use the design chart to determine what color beads to use. String two beads. PNT the loop of thread that connects the beads in the previous row. PNBT second bead strung on and pull tight. *String one bead. PNT the loop of thread that connects the beads in the previous round. PNBT strung bead and pull tight.* See Fig. 2. Repeat between asterisks until the end of the round. Always start the round with two beads instead of one so the thread won't pass on the outside of the first bead.

At the end of every round, PNDT the first bead of the round and PNUT the second bead. Now you are ready to begin the next round. See Fig. 3.

ROUNDS 2–53: Same as Round 1, changing colors of beads according to the design chart.

Line up the design in the center front of bag and flatten. If you have enough thread left over, use it to sew up the bottom. If not, anchor a new thread to the body of the bag. Work the thread to one of the bottom sides and sew. Pass needle under thread loop between the first two beads and then under the loop on the opposite side. Continue until the end. Then sew up one more time, going back over what you just sewed, to strengthen it. Leave thread end to use on fringe if it's long enough.

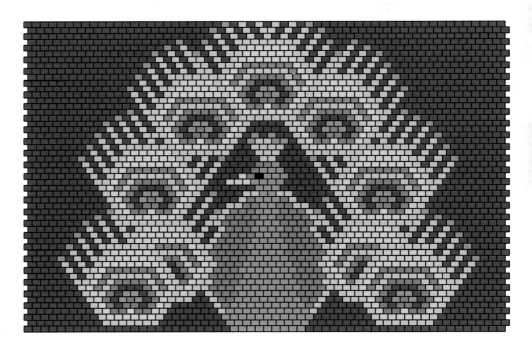

■ Silver-lined violet
■ Semi-matte medium blue
■ Matte transparent Kelly green
□ Lined lime green
■ Lined topaz
□ Silver-lined gold
■ Black

Design Chart

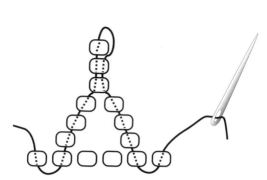

Figure 4

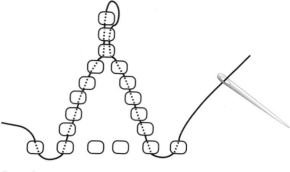

Figure 5

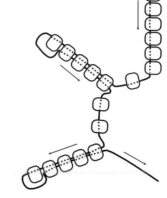

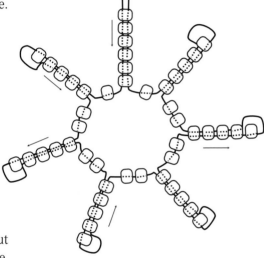

Figure 6

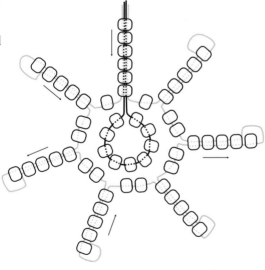

Figure 7

■ Edging

Create the edging at the top of the bag using the second needle and thread. Start with front edging. See Fig. 4. * String three purple beads, two blue beads, and one gold. PNBT the two blue beads and then string on three purple beads. PNDT the third bead from the bead that the thread came out of on top round of the bag. PNUT the adjacent bead on top of the bag.* Repeat between asterisks until last bead of the front of bag.

The back top edging is basically the same as the front top edging, except you use more beads to make a taller edging. See Fig. 5. *String five purple beads, two blue beads, and one gold bead. PNBT the two blue beads and then string five purple beads. PNDT third bead from where strung beads are coming out and then PNUT adjacent bead.* Repeat between asterisks until the end of the back of the bag. Weave end back through body of work.

■ Fringe

Thread needle onto 5' length of thread. Weave through work to anchor it and bring needle out through bead at the bottom left edge of bag.

There are thirty-five strands of fringe, one for every bead along bottom of bag.

STRAND 1: String three lime-green beads, one Kelly green, one blue, one Kelly green, three lime green, one gold, four lime green, and one blue. PNBT four lime-green beads. This forms one finger of feather fringe. *String 2 gold beads, 4 lime green, 1 blue. PNBT 4 lime-green beads.* See Fig. 6. Repeat between asterisks four more times for a total of six fingers. PNBT three lime-green beads, one Kelly green, one blue, one Kelly green, and three lime-green beads. See Fig. 7. PNUT bead on bottom of bag to the left of where strand came out and then PNDT the bead where the strand is coming out. PNBT strand of lime-green beads, Kelly green beads, and blue bead so that the needle is coming out of the middle of the top of the circle of beads. String three purple beads, three blue beads, and three more purple beads. PNBT the strand of lime-green, Kelly green, and blue bead. PNUT bead on bottom of bag directly above the strand. PNDT the next bead on the bottom of the bag. See Fig. 8.

This forms the peacock feather strand. There are six of them in the fringe, three on each side of the middle of the bag, with increasingly more beads in each strand as you move towards the middle.

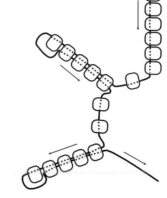

Figure 8

STRAND 2: *String two blue beads, three Kelly green beads, one gold bead. PNBT three Kelly green beads.* Repeat between asterisks two more times for a total of three fingers on strand. Then string two blue beads and one gold bead. PNBT all the blue beads. PNUT the bead on the body of bag directly on top of the strand. PNDT the next bead.

STRAND 3: Same as Strand 2, except use purple beads for the blue beads and topaz beads for the green ones.

STRAND 4: This is another peacock feather strand. Work same as Strand 1, except instead of stringing on three lime-green beads on either side of Kelly green bead, blue bead, Kelly green bead, string on five lime-green beads (this is the part of the strand that is above the circular feather part) so that this feather strand is longer than Strand 1.

STRAND 5: Same as Strand 2, except make five green fingers instead of three.

STRAND 6: Same as Strand 3, except make five topaz fingers instead of three.

STRAND 7: Same as Strand 4, except string eight lime-green beads on either side of Kelly green, blue, and Kelly green.

STRAND 8: String twenty-six purple beads and five gold beads. This forms a small gold ring at the end of the strand. PNBT all purple beads and PNUT bead on bottom of body of bag. PNDT next bead on body of bag.

STRAND 9: String thirty-five purple beads and five topaz beads. PNBT all purple beads. PNUT bead on bottom of body of bag. PNDT next bead on body of bag.

STRAND 10: Same as Strand 8, except string thirty-nine purple

beads instead of twenty-six.

STRAND 11: Same as Strand 9, except string forty-five purple beads instead of thirty-five.

STRAND 12: String forty-eight lime-green beads and five gold beads. PNBT all green beads, PNUT bead on body of bag that is directly above strand, and then PNDT next bead on body of bag.

STRAND 13: Same as Strand 12, except string fifty Kelly green beads and five topaz.

STRAND 14: Same as Strand 12, except string fifty-two blue beads and five gold beads.

STRAND 15: String fifty-six blue beads and five topaz.

STRAND 16: String fifty-nine blue beads and five gold.

STRAND 17: This is the peacock foot strand. String three blue beads, twelve topaz beads, and one lime-green bead. PNBT three topaz beads. String four topaz beads and one lime-green bead. PNBT three topaz beads. String three topaz beads and one lime-green bead. PNBT three topaz beads. String three topaz beads and one lime-green bead. PNBT three topaz beads. These are the four toes of the peacock. String forty-seven blue beads and five topaz. PNBT all forty-seven blue beads, topaz beads of leg (not toes), and three blue beads. PNUT bead on body of bag that is directly above strand and then PNDT next bead on body of bag.

STRAND 18: Same as Strand 16, except string sixty-two blue beads.

STRAND 19: Same as Strand 17.

STRAND 20: Same as Strand 16.

STRAND 21: Same as Strand 15.

STRAND 22: Same as Strand 14.

STRAND 23: Same as Strand 13.

STRAND 24: Same as Strand 12.

STRAND 25: Same as Strand 11.

STRAND 26: Same as Strand 10.

STRAND 27: Same as Strand 9.

STRAND 28: Same as Strand 8.

STRAND 29: Same as Strand 7.

STRAND 30: Same as Strand 6.

STRAND 31: Same as Strand 5.

STRAND 32: Same as Strand 4.

STRAND 33: Same as Strand 3.

STRAND 34: Same as Strand 2.

STRAND 35: Same as Strand 1.

Weave in ends.

■ Necklace

Use two strands of thread about 3' long. Thread a needle to each length of thread. Pass both needles up through the bead at the top edge where you want the necklace to start. Leave thread ends about 6" long to later separate and weave back into the work. String onto both needles **eight purple beads, *one gold, one topaz, one Kelly green, one lime green, one Kelly green, one topaz, one gold. Now string forty purple beads on one needle and forty blue beads on the other needle.* Repeat between single asterisks two more times. Then string onto both needles one gold, one topaz, one Kelly green, one lime green, one Kelly green, one topaz, one gold, eight purple beads.** String 160 gold beads to both needles for the back of the necklace. Repeat between double asterisks for the other side of the necklace. Pass both needles through bead at top of bag on other side. Weave in the four thread ends separately.

Parrot Feather Amulet Bag Necklace

Ellen Talbott

This little feather amulet bag may not let you fly like a parrot, but your spirits will soar while wearing it around your neck.

The finished piece measures 1" x 5" including fringe.

MATERIALS

1 oz light pale green seed beads, size 11°

One hundred and three transparent iridescent gold seed beads, size 11°

One hundred and two turquoise white heart seed beads, size 11°

Ninety-eight medium pale green seed beads, size 11°

Sixty-six transparent green seed beads, size 11°

Thirty-two iridescent opaque yellow seed beads, size 11°

Thirteen transparent red seed beads, size 11°

Forty-five 1/2" iridescent blue-green bugle beads, size 5

Seventeen malachite chips

Fourteen transparent blue seed beads, size 6°

Eleven transparent dark red seed beads, size 6°

Ten transparent green seed beads, size 6°

Two 1/2" transparent red oblong beads

Two gold bugle beads, size 5°

White nylon beading thread, size D

Two beading needles, size #12

Scissors

Pliers

Thread two needles on either end of a length of thread about 5' long. Use this to make a ladder stitch band twenty-four bugle beads long. Sort your bugle beads so that the ones you choose are the same length and don't have obvious chips on the outer edges. After making the band, connect the first and last beads to form a cylinder. This cylinder is the base from which you will build the body of the bag. Use one needle now to make the body of the bag and the other needle to create the edge at the top of the bag later.

Body of the Bag

Using the brick stitch, make a round of twenty-four light pale green beads. These beads will be used as the background color. Use two beads instead of one for the beginning of every round. To finish a round, PNDT the first bead in the round and PNUT the second bead. See Fig. 1. Now you are ready to begin the next round.

For the second round, follow the design chart. It doesn't matter where you start the design on the bag, because at the end when you sew up the bottom of the bag you can center the design where you want it. Work the bag from the top down by following design chart from top to bottom. Work forty-three rounds from the design chart and then for the last round use the light pale green beads of the background. Now you are ready to sew up the bottom of the bag. Line up the design in the center front of the bag and flatten it. If you have enough thread on your needle, use it to sew up the bottom of the bag. If not, add new thread. Work your needle through the beads to one side of the bottom of the bag and begin to sew. To sew, pass the needle under the loop of thread

between the first two beads and then under the loop on the opposite side. Continue to the end. Sew up one more time, going back over what you just sewed. Weave excess thread back up through work and cut.

Next, create the edge at the top of the bag. Using the second needle, make a round of light pale green beads in the brick stitch. For the second round, use six green seed beads, size 6°, and six blue seed beads, size 6°. Alternate the green beads with the blue ones, using every other loop of thread from the light pale green round to compensate for the larger size of the beads. See Fig. 2. At the end of the round, weave excess thread back into work and cut.

Fringe

Thread your needle with a 5' strand of thread. Weave the thread through the work to secure the end, and bring the needle out through the bead at the bottom edge of the bag. Next string three gold beads, one red seed bead (size 6°), one buglebead, one malachite chip, and one light pale green seed bead. PNBT malachite chip, bugle bead, red bead, and three gold beads. Now PNUT the

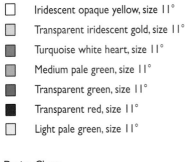

- ☐ Iridescent opaque yellow, size 11°
- ☐ Transparent iridescent gold, size 11°
- ☐ Turquoise white heart, size 11°
- ☐ Medium pale green, size 11°
- ☐ Transparent green, size 11°
- ■ Transparent red, size 11°
- ☐ Light pale green, size 11°

Design Chart

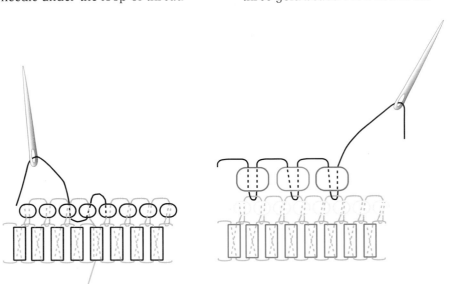

Figure 1

Figure 2

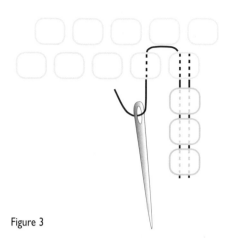

Figure 3

bead on the bottom edge of bag again, and PNDT the adjacent bead. See Fig. 3.

Continue in this manner until there are eleven strands of fringe. Follow the fringe chart for bead pattern. When finished, weave excess thread into body of work and cut.

■ Necklace

Use a double strand of thread for the necklace. Cut a length of thread that is 62" long. Place the needle in the center of the thread, and bring the needle up through the bugle bead and the top edge beads that are closest to the edge of the bag where you want the necklace to start. Leave a tail of the thread ends about 6" long. You will weave these back into the work separately later.

To create one side of the necklace, string five iridescent yellow seed beads, one red oblong bead, one gold bugle bead, one green seed bead (size 6°), two blue seed beads (size 6°), one blue-green bugle bead, one malachite chip, one turquoise seed bead, one medium pale green seed bead, one turquoise seed bead, one malachite chip, one turquoise seed bead, one medium pale green seed bead, one turquoise seed bead, one malachite chip, one blue-green bugle bead, two blue seed beads (size 6°), one green seed bead (size 6°), eleven medium pale green seed beads, seven turquoise seed beads, five transparent green seed beads, five light pale green seed beads, one blue-green bugle bead, five light pale green seed beads, one blue-green bugle bead, five light pale green seed beads, and one blue-green bugle bead.

To create the back of the necklace, string 12" of light pale green seed beads.

Working backwards, repeat the instructions for the first side of the necklace. You should end up with two matching sides. When you are done stringing the beads, PNDT the top bead of the bag at the opposite side from where you started the necklace. PNDT the closest bugle bead and separate threads. Weave each one through the body of the work to secure them. Do the same with the thread ends on the other side of the bag.

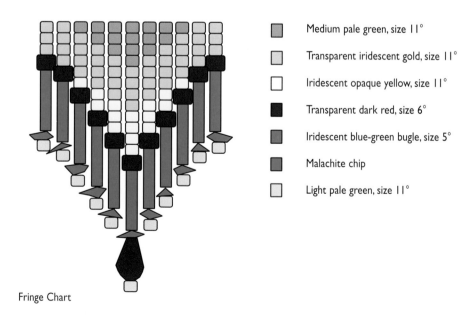

Fringe Chart

▨	Medium pale green, size 11°
▨	Transparent iridescent gold, size 11°
☐	Iridescent opaque yellow, size 11°
■	Transparent dark red, size 6°
▨	Iridescent blue-green bugle, size 5°
▨	Malachite chip
☐	Light pale green, size 11°

A Day in the Park: Miniature Picnic Basket, Wine Bottle, Loaf of Bread, and Tablecloth

Elizabeth Gourley

The ants would love this picnic. It's just their size! With its woven look, the herringbone stitch is perfect for a basket. It will fool more than the ants. You might have to do a double-take to make sure it's not really a fiber basket. Complete it with a checkered tablecloth, loaf of bread, and wine bottle and you'll just have to find a friend for a delightful day in the park.

The finished dimensions of the pieces are:

Basket: 2" long x 1¹/₄" wide x 2¹/₄" tall including handle.

Wine bottle: 1¹/₂" tall x ³/₈" at its widest point.

Loaf of bread: 1¹/₂" long x ¹/₂" wide x ¹/₄" tall.

Tablecloth: 2" x 1⁵/₈".

The tablecloth and basket are done in the herringbone stitch, but the bottle and bread are done in peyote.

■ Basket

MATERIALS

10 grams Japanese tubular beads, dyed opaque matte chestnut, Delica #794

4 grams Japanese tubular beads, matte emerald, Delica #859

Two ³/₁₆" long greenish beads for basket closures

Black or brown nylon beading thread, size D

Beading needle, size 12

Scissors

Detail of Miniature Picnic Basket

Once you get the herringbone stitch mastered, this project will quickly take shape. It is basically five flat rectangles sewn together (with two flat rectangles attached as the flip lids) and, of course, a handle.

Start with the long sides of the basket. Using doubled thread, string twenty-four beads in this pattern: one green bead, two brown beads, two green beads, two brown beads, two green beads, two brown beads, two green beads, two brown beads, two green beads, two brown beads, two green beads, two brown beads, two green beads, two brown beads, and one green bead.

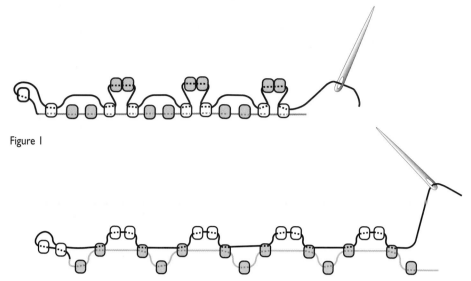

Figure 1

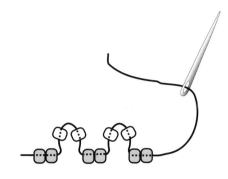

Figure 2

Figure 3

ROW 1: String one brown bead. PNT green bead. Skip the next two brown beads. PNT first green bead of two-bead set. String two brown beads. PNT second green bead of two-bead set. *Skip two brown beads. PNT first green bead of two-bead set. String two brown beads. PNT second green bead of two-bead set.* Repeat between asterisks until the end of the row. See Fig. 1.

ROW 2: String one brown and one green bead. PNBT brown bead. *PNT first brown bead of next two-bead set. String on two green beads. PNT second brown bead of two-bead set. Skip one green bead.* Repeat between asterisks until the end of the row. Every other two-bead set will be hanging down on this row. Therefore, you have to scoot the beads so that they are on top of the thread and ready to have the needle pass through them. This only happens on Row 2. See Fig. 2.

ROW 3: String one green bead and one brown bead. PNBT green bead. *PNT the first bead of the next two-bead set. String two brown beads. PNT second bead of the two-bead set.* Repeat between the asterisks until the end of the row.

As you have probably noticed by now, the beads of each row are not in a straight line in the herringbone stitch. Each group of two makes an inverted U shape. When pulling your stitches tight, especially with the matte Japanese tubular beads, make sure one bead is on one side of the U and one is on the other. See Fig. 3.

ROW 4: String on one brown bead and then one green bead. PNBT brown bead. *PNT the first bead of the next two-bead set. String two green beads. PNT second bead of two-bead set.* Repeat between asterisks until the end of the row.

ROW 5: String one green bead and one brown bead. PNBT green bead. *PNT first bead of next two-bead set. String two brown beads. PNT second bead of two-bead set.* Repeat between asterisks until the end of the row.

ROWS 6-13: Work with brown beads in herringbone stitch.

Finishing edge: To form an even edge for the bottom of the basket, string one brown bead. PNT next two-bead set. *String one brown bead. PNT next two-bead set.* Repeat between asterisks until the end of the row. See Fig. 4. Leave thread end long for sewing the sides together.

Make two of these long sides. After you have finished the two long sides, complete the two shorter sides.

Short Sides

Double the thread. String sixteen beads in the one green, two brown, two green, etc., pattern. Last bead is one green. Follow the same instructions as the long sides for thirteen rows. Make two.

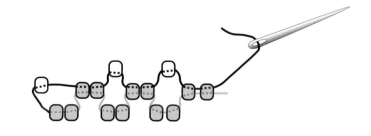

Figure 4

Bottom of Basket

Using doubled thread, string sixteen brown beads. Work in herringbone stitch with brown beads for thirty-four rows.

Sew the sides and bottom together by weaving thread through every other bead back and forth from one edge to the other of the two pieces you're sewing together. The piece seems wobbly at this point, but it will be sturdier as you finish.

Handle of Basket

Using doubled thread, string four beads in this pattern: one green bead, one brown bead, one brown bead, one green bead.

ROW 1: String one green bead. PNT last green bead strung. String two brown beads. PNT next green bead.

ROW 2: String two green beads. PNBT first green bead strung. PNT first brown bead. String two brown beads. PNT next brown bead. PNT last green bead.

ROW 3: Same as Row 2. See Fig. 5.

Repeat Row 2 for a total of fifty-two rows.

Using doubled thread about 6' long, find the middle of one long side of basket. Sew basket handle on top edge of side. PNT all the green beads on one side of the handle, then sew handle to top edge of middle of other long side. When secure, PNT all the green beads on the other side of the handle. This will help reinforce the handle. At this point, you can also reinforce the top edge of the basket by PNT all the top edge beads. With the same thread, come out on the inside of the basket under the middle of the handle. String twenty-two brown beads to make the bar for anchoring the flaps. See Fig. 6. Sew the twenty-two bead strand to the opposite side of the basket, making sure it's in the middle of the side. PNBT the twenty-two beads two more times so that the strand is somewhat stiff. Weave in the end.

Basket Flaps

Using doubled black thread, string sixteen brown beads.

ROW 1: String one brown bead. PNBT the sixteenth bead strung. *Skip two beads and PNT next bead. String two brown beads. PNT next bead.* Repeat between asterisks to finish row.

ROW 2: String two brown beads. PNBT first bead strung. *Skip one bead and PNT next bead. String two green beads. PNT next bead.* Repeat between asterisks until the end of the row.

ROW 3: String two brown beads. PNBT first bead strung. PNT first bead of next two-bead set. String one green bead and one brown bead. PNT second bead of two-bead set. *PNT first bead of next two-bead set. String two brown beads. PNT second bead of two-bead set.* Repeat between asterisks until last stitch, then string one brown and one green bead. PNT last bead. The green beads form the stripe around the edge of the flap.

Repeat Row 3 twelve more times for a total of fifteen rows.

ROW 16: Decrease one bead at the beginning of the row. To do this, do not string on two beads; just PNT first green bead. Work the rest of the row the same as Row 3.

ROWS 17–18: Same as Row 16.

ROW 19: Finishing edge. PNT first two beads. *String one brown bead. PNT next two beads.* Repeat between asterisks until the end of the row. Make two flaps.

Using double thread, reinforce edges of flaps by PNT all edge beads. Now sew flaps to the bar of beads in the middle of the basket. PNT two edge beads of flap. Then PNT two beads of middle bar. Skip two beads on flap and then PNT next two beads. Skip two beads on bar, then PNT next two beads. Repeat until entire edge of flap is connected. Do the same for other flap on opposite side of bar.

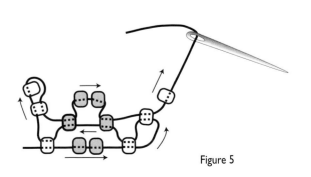

Figure 5

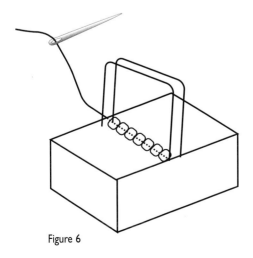

Figure 6

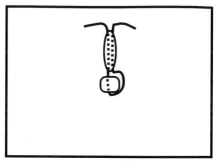

Figure 7

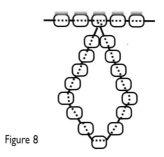

Figure 8

Detail of tablecloth

Basket Clasp

Do not double thread for this step. Secure one end of the thread on the short side of the basket by bringing the needle out of the middle bead in the top brown stripe of the basket side. String green clasp bead and one green bead. PNBT clasp bead. PNT other brown middle bead and then weave in the end. See Fig. 7.

On the flap, secure the thread and come out of the bead on the front edge in the middle of the flap. String fifteen brown beads. PNT other brown middle bead and then weave in the end. See Fig. 8. Repeat on other side.

■ Checkered Tablecloth

M A T E R I A L S
....

4 grams Japanese tubular beads, dyed matte transparent red, Delica #774

4 grams Japanese tubular beads, Ceylon light yellow (off-white), Delica #203

White nylon beading thread, size D

Beading needle, size 12

Scissors

Using about 4' of white thread, string twenty-four beads in this pattern: one white bead, *two red beads, two white beads.* Repeat between asterisks until last bead, which is one white bead. Leave a 6" tail of thread and hold tight so that the beads won't slip off the end before you finish the first row.

ROW 1: String one white bead. PNT next white bead. Skip two red beads. PNT next white bead. String two red beads. PNT next white bead. *Skip two red beads, then PNT next white bead. String two red beads. PNT next white bead.* Repeat until last white bead, which you PNT. See Fig. 1.

ROW 2: String two white beads. PNBT first white bead strung. Skip one bead, then PNT first bead of next two-bead set. String two red beads. PNT second bead of two-bead set. *Skip one bead, then PNT next white bead. String two white beads. PNT other white bead. Skip one bead. PNT next red bead. String on two red beads. PNT next red bead.* Repeat between asterisks until the end of the row. PNT last bead of row. This row is awkward, but once you get past it, the rest is much easier. You might have to adjust the thread tension by loosening the row. See Fig. 2.

ROW 3: String two red beads. PNBT first red bead strung. *PNT first bead of next two-bead set. String two white beads. PNT last bead of two-bead set. PNT first bead of next two-bead set. String on two red beads. PNT last bead of two-bead set.* Repeat between asterisks until the end of the row. PNT last bead of row.

ROW 4: String two white beads. PNBT first white bead strung. *PNT first bead of next two-bead set.

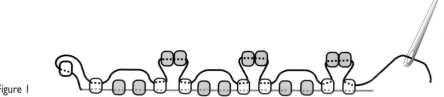

Figure 1

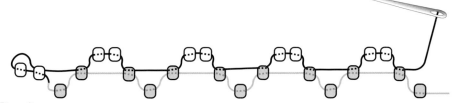

Figure 2

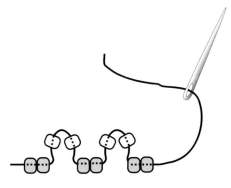
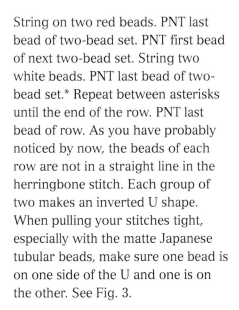

Figure 3

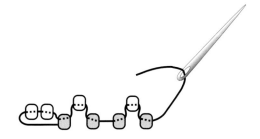

Figure 4

String on two red beads. PNT last bead of two-bead set. PNT first bead of next two-bead set. String two white beads. PNT last bead of two-bead set.* Repeat between asterisks until the end of the row. PNT last bead of row. As you have probably noticed by now, the beads of each row are not in a straight line in the herringbone stitch. Each group of two makes an inverted U shape. When pulling your stitches tight, especially with the matte Japanese tubular beads, make sure one bead is on one side of the U and one is on the other. See Fig. 3.

ROW 5: Same as Row 4.

ROWS 6–7: Same as Row 3.

Now follow the red-and-white checkered pattern for a total of thirty-two rows.

ROW 33: Work in all red beads.

Ending row: String two white beads. PNT first red bead. String one white bead. *PNT next two red beads. String one white bead.* Repeat between asterisks until the end of the row. See Fig 4. Weave in the ends until they are secure.

■ Wine Bottle

The wine bottle is done in the tubular peyote stitch. You begin with the cork at the top of the bottle.

MATERIALS

2 grams Japanese tubular beads, dyed matte transparent Kelly green, Delica #776
Thirty-one Japanese tubular beads, Ceylon light yellow (off-white), Delica #203
Eighteen Japanese tubular beads, matte light brown, Delica #853
Black nylon beading thread, size D
Beading needle, size 12

ROUND 1: Using about 3' of black-thread, string three brown beads. PNBT first bead strung to form a circle.

ROUND 2: *String one brown bead. PNT next bead of previous round.* Repeat between asterisks two times for a total of three brown beads. See Fig. 1.

Detail of wine bottle

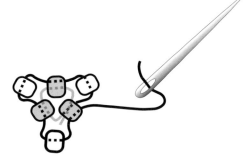

Figure I

Figure 2

ROUND 3: This round is done in brown beads. PNT first bead of Round 2 and next bead from Round 1. *String one bead. PNT next bead from Round 1, making sure that the strung bead is on top of the bead from Round 2.* See Fig. 2. Repeat between asterisks twice more.

ROUND 4: This round is also done in brown beads. PNT first bead of Round 3. *String one bead. PNT next bead.* Repeat between asterisks twice more.

ROUND 5: PNT first bead of Round 4. Using brown beads, *string 2 beads. PNT next bead of Round 4.* Repeat between asterisks twice more, making sure the thread tension is kept tight.

ROUND 6: PNT first two beads of Round 5. *String one green bead. PNT next two beads.* Repeat between asterisks twice more.

ROUND 7: PNT first bead of Round 6. *String two green beads. PNT next bead.* Repeat between asterisks twice more.

Repeat Rounds 6 and 7 with green beads until Round 20 (total of fourteen rounds of green beads). It is important to tighten the thread tension after every round.

ROUND 20: This is the increase round that flares out the base of the bottle. PNT first two beads of Round 19. *String one green bead. PNT first bead of next two-bead set. String one green bead. PNT last bead of two-bead set.* Repeat between aster-

isks twice more for a total of six green beads on this round.

ROUND 21: PNT first bead from Round 20. *String two green beads. PNT next bead from Round 20.* Repeat between asterisks until the end of the round.

ROUND 22: PNT first two beads from Round 21. *String one green bead. PNT next two beads from Round 21.* Repeat between asterisks until the end of the round.

Repeat Rounds 21 and 22 for ten rounds until Round 31.

ROUND 31: This is the starting round for the white label. PNT first two beads of Round 30. *String one white bead. PNT next two-bead set.* Repeat between asterisks twice more. String one green bead. PNT next two-bead set. Finish round using green beads.

ROUND 32: *PNT first white bead. String two white beads. PNT next white bead.* Repeat between asterisks once more. String two green beads. PNT next bead. Repeat, using green beads until the end of the round.

Continue using white beads for the label. Keep the label square for a total of nine rounds.

ROUNDS 40–44: Work the same as the rest of the bottle using only green beads. Round 44 will be the foot of the bottle.

ROUND 45: This round is the start of the flat bottom of the bottle. Don't PNT the first two beads from Round 44 as you normally do. Instead, string one green bead. PNT next bead from Round 43. String one green bead. PNT next bead from Round 43. Continue in this manner until the end of the round.

ROUND 46: PNT first bead from Round 45. String one green bead.

PNT next two beads from Round 45 (decrease). Repeat between asterisks two more times (total of three beads).

ROUND 47: Finishing round. String one green bead. PNT first bead of previous round. Repeat two more times. PNBT first bead of Round 47 and pull thread tight. Weave in loose ends.

■ Loaf of Bread

This project is done in the peyote stitch.

MATERIALS

4 grams Japanese tubular beads, matte cantaloupe, Delica #852
Fifteen Japanese tubular beads, Ceylon light yellow (off-white), Delica #203
White nylon beading thread, size D
Beading needle, size 12
Scissors

Detail of loaf of bread

ROWS 1–3: String twenty-four brown beads. String one brown bead. PNT second brown bead. String one brown bead. Skip a bead and then PNT next bead. String one brown bead. Skip a bead, then PNT next bead. Repeat until the end of the row. See Fig. 1.

ROW 4: String one brown bead. PNT first bead that is sticking up (Row 3). String one brown bead. PNT next bead from Row 3 (sticking up). Repeat until the end of the row using brown beads (total of twelve beads).

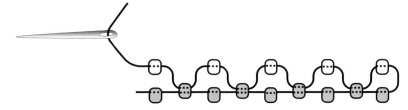

Figure 1

ROW 5: Increase one brown bead at beginning of row by stringing two beads and then PNT first bead strung. See Fig. 2. Follow peyote stitch with brown beads until the end of the row.

ROW 6: Same as Row 5.

ROW 7–8: Do not increase. Work brown beads in peyote stitch.

ROW 9: Decrease one bead at the beginning of row by PNT first bead. Then string one brown bead. Work the rest of row in peyote stitch.

ROW 10–12: Same as Row 9.

ROW 13: This row starts the rounded top of the loaf of bread. It is worked on the top of the flat bottom you just completed. String one brown bead. PNT second bead of Row 11, making sure that you keep the flat bottom of the loaf horizontal and bead just strung on on top of the Row 11 beads. String one brown bead and PNT next bead of Row 11. See Fig. 3. Repeat in this manner until you get to the last bead of Row 11. PNT last bead of Row 11. To begin the curve around the end of the loaf, string one brown bead, then PNT first bead of Row 9. String one brown bead and PNT first bead of Row 7. String one brown bead. PNT first bead of Row 4. String one brown bead. PNT second bead of Row 2. To finish Row 13, work with the beads of Row 2 in peyote stitch, repeating what you did on the beads of Row 11. To begin the curve around the end of the loaf, string one brown bead. PNT first bead of Row 4. String one brown

bead. PNT first bead of Row 7. String one brown bead. PNT first bead of Row 9. Now you have formed a row of beads on top of the bottom part of the loaf.

ROW 14: PNT first bead of Row 13. String one brown bead. PNT next bead of Row 13. Work the brown beads in peyote stitch for the rest of the row, which goes all around the loaf.

ROW 15: Same as 14, except decrease one bead at each end of the loaf. To decrease, PNT two beads at the ends of the loaf, instead of one bead.

ROW 16: PNT first bead of Row 15. String one white bead. PNT next bead. String one brown bead. PNT next bead. String one brown bead. PNT next bead. String one white bead. PNT next bead. String brown beads for next three stitches, then string one white bead. Use brown beads for next three stitches, then PNT next two beads. String one brown bead. PNT next bead. String one white bead. PNT next bead. String brown beads for next three stitches, then string one white bead. String brown beads for the next two stitches, and then one white bead. String brown beads for the next three stitches, then PNT for next two beads. String brown beads for the last two stitches.

ROW 17: PNT white bead. String one white bead for next stitch. String brown beads for next two stitches. String one white bead for next stitch.

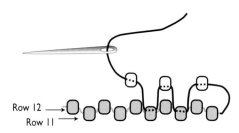

Row 12 →
Row 11 →

Figure 3

String brown beads for next three stitches. String one white bead for next stitch. String brown beads for next two stitches. PNT next bead from Row 15 and then the next bead from Row 16. String one brown bead. PNT next bead. String one white bead for next stitch. String brown beads for next three stitches. Then string one white bead. String brown beads for next two stitches. Then string one white bead. String brown beads for next two stitches. Then PNT next bead from Row 15 and the next bead from Row 16. String brown beads for next two stitches.

ROW 18: Finishing. Sew sides of loaf together to form a solid top. This is accomplished by PNT interlocking beads from each side and pulling tight. This will close up the top of the loaf and the seam will be invisible. See Fig. 4.

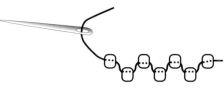

Figure 4

A Touch of the Rainforest: Poison Arrow Frog Barrette

Elizabeth Gourley

With the colorful poison arrow frog that adorns this barrette, you will feel as if you just stepped into the rainforest. It is done in the versatile square stitch, which lends itself well to making free forms.

The finished piece measures 4" x 2¹/₂".

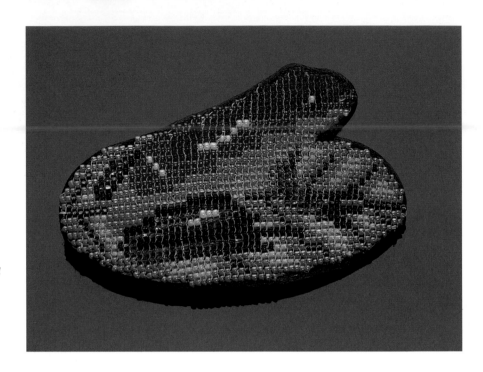

MATERIALS

Seventeen white seed beads, size 11°

Forty-three black seed beads, size 11°

2 grams lined translucent dark red seed beads, size 11°

2 grams opaque red seed beads, size 11°

2 grams opaque orange seed beads, size 11°

2 grams translucent bright yellow seed beads, size 11°

2 grams translucent cobalt-blue seed beads, size 11°

2 grams lined translucent light blue seed beads, size 11°

2 grams translucent mint-green seed beads, size 11°

2 grams opaque medium green seed beads, size 11°

2 grams lined translucent dark green seed beads, size 11°

White nylon beading thread, size D

6" x 6" piece of ¹/₈" cowhide leather

1 yd of dark blue edging cord

One 3" long barrette finding

Beading needle, size 12

Leather glue

Leather matte knife

Scissors

In order to have as few increases as possible (it's much easier to decrease), start beading on the widest row, Row 11. (Row 1 is the bottom of the graph.) Work from Row 11 down to Row 1. When done, work Rows 12–29.

ROW 11: String fifty-seven beads according to the color scheme of the design chart from left to right. Leave a long tail of thread and hold secure-ly it so that the beads won't slip off. Don't make a knot so that the first row can be adjusted.

ROW 10: Work in square stitch, reading the design chart from right to left. String two beads. PNT second bead on first row with needle point-ing in the opposite direction of the row. PNBT the second bead strung and pull tight. String on one bead. PNT next bead in first row with nee-dle pointing the opposite way of the row. PNBT bead you just strung. Pull tight. Continue until the end of the row. See Fig. 1.

ROWS 9–11: Work in square stitch. Decrease according to design chart. Read the chart, switching from left to right and right to left every other row. Weave in end of thread .

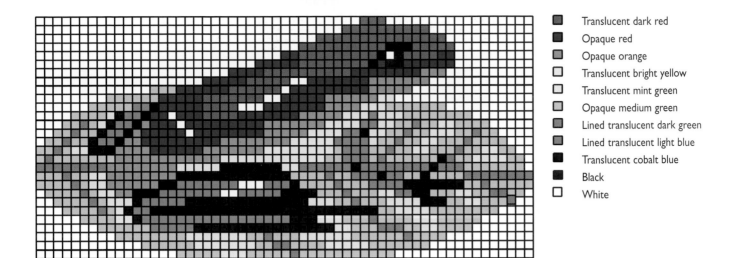

Design Chart

Translucent dark red
Opaque red
Opaque orange
Translucent bright yellow
Translucent mint green
Opaque medium green
Lined translucent dark green
Lined translucent light blue
Translucent cobalt blue
Black
White

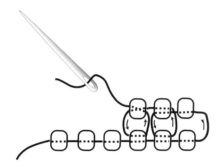

Figure 1

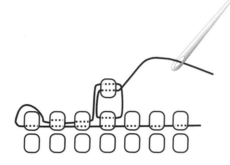

Figure 2

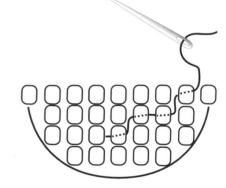

Figure 3

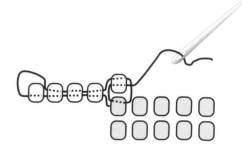

Figure 4

Decrease: To decrease, PNBT second bead from the end and bring out the needle next to the bead that is directly under the first bead in the row you're starting. Then start row with the square stitch. See Fig. 2. To decrease one bead at the beginning of the row, simply PNBT second bead from the end and then begin the first stich. To decrease at the end of the row, simply stop where the row ends.

Turn piece around. Secure the thread in body of work by positioning thread so that it comes out of the second-to-last bead on right side of Row 11. See Fig. 3.

ROWS 12–29: Start on Row 12 of design chart, working in square stitch from right to left. Decrease on edges of every row except Rows 20–24, where you increase on right side edges for frog's nose.

Increase: To increase at end of row, string the desired number of beads and, on the next row, treat them as if they had been square-stitched. To increase at the beginning of the row, string on desired number of beads. PNBT the beads, skipping the last bead strung. Now start the row as normal. See Fig. 4.

■ Finishing

Trace the outline of the finished frog onto paper. Cut out and place on leather. Using a leather matte knife, cut the leather to the shape of the frog. Glue beads to leather, making sure the beads cover the whole sur-

face of the leather. I glued the beads to the rough side of the leather so the back would be smooth. Cut a piece of the blue cord long enough to go around the perimeter of the leather. Glue onto the edge of leather. I started and ended under the frog's chin, cutting the cord at an angle so that the ends fit together. Glue barrette finding to middle of back of frog.

Goldfish Earrings

Ellen Talbott

Inspired by the goldfish swimming in the pond of my backyard, these unusual earrings are done in the square stitch. They are quick and easy to do.

The finished piece measures 2" x ³/4".

MATERIALS

2 grams Japanese tubular beads, black, Delica #010
2 grams Japanese tubular beads, silver-lined sapphire, Delica #047
2 grams Japanese tubular beads, semi-matte silver-lined medium green, Delica #688
2 grams Japanese tubular beads, semi-matte silver-lined squash, Delica #681
2 grams Japanese tubular beads, semi-matte silver-lined orange, Delica #682
2 grams Japanese tubular beads, semi-matte silver-lined dark ruby, Delica #683
Six green round, flat drop beads
Black nylon beading thread, size D
One beading needle, size #10
Two gold-colored ear wires
Scissors

ROW 1: String five beads according to the design chart. To read the chart, start with the first row at the bottom of the chart and read from left to right. For the second row, read from right to left. For the third row, read left to right, and so on. Don't tie a knot at the end of the thread, because the tension may need to be adjusted. If the tension is too tight, the work will curl. Leave a tail of thread long enough to weave back into work later.

ROW 2: String on a black bead and an orange bead. PNBT the last black bead on the first row and back through the orange bead. This will increase the second row by one bead. See Fig. 1. Continue the row, following the design chart with the square stitch.

ROW 3: Work the first six beads in square stitch, then string the five remaining black beads.

ROW 4: String two black beads and PNBT last bead on Row 3. See Fig. 2. Then PNT second bead on fourth

■ Black
■ Semi-matte silver-lined dark ruby
■ Semi-matte silver-lined orange
□ Semi-matte silver-lined squash

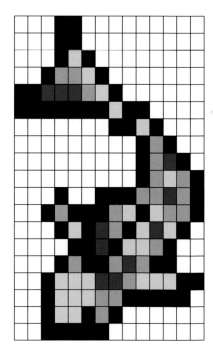

Design Chart

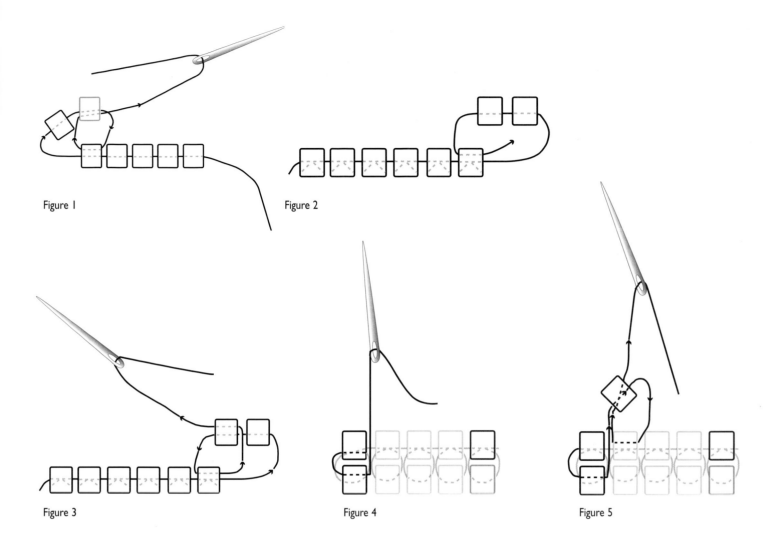

Figure 1

Figure 2

Figure 3

Figure 4

Figure 5

row. See Fig. 3. Pull tight and continue in square stitch until end of row.

ROW 5: Decrease one stitch at the beginning of the row by PNT the last bead on the previous row and bringing thread back up between the two outermost beads in the row just completed. See Fig. 4. String one black bead, PNT the second-to-last bead on Row 4, and PNBT the bead just added on. Pull tight. See Fig. 5. Continue to follow design chart in square stitch to end of the row.

ROW 6: Work in square stitch following design chart until end of row.

ROW 7: Increase one bead at the beginning of the row. To increase, string two beads, then PNBT last bead on Row 6, and then PNT second bead on Row 7. See Figs. 2 and 3.

ROW 8: String two beads, then PNT last bead on Row 7, and then back through second bead on Row 8. See Fig. 6. Pull tight. Continue in square stitch, following design chart to the end of the row.

ROW 9: String one black bead and PNT second bead from end of Row 8. Then PNBT first bead on Row 9. Next, PNT third and fourth beads from the end on Row 8 to create the two-bead space between the tip of the fin and the body of the fish. See Fig. 7. Continue in the square stitch to the end of the row.

ROW 10: Work in square stitch following design chart.

ROW 11: Work in square stitch following design chart.

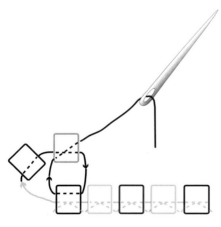

Figure 6

ROW 12: Decrease one bead at beginning of row. See Figs. 4 and 5. Continue in square stitch following the design chart.

ROW 13: Increase two beads by stringing two beads and then PNBT the second bead. See Fig. 8. Pull tight. Work last two beads in the square stitch.

ROW 14: Decrease one bead and work three beads in the square stitch. Then string seven black beads.

ROW 15: Work in square stitch until end of row. Be aware of the thread tension on the seven added beads in Row 14. They will have a tendency to move around at first.

ROW 16: Decrease one bead and continue in square stitch to end of row.

ROW 17: Decrease one bead and continue in square stitch to end of row.

ROW 18: Decrease one bead and work two black beads in square stitch.

ROW 19: Work two black beads in square stitch.

To create a loop of beads to attach to the ear wires, string on six squash beads and PNT ear wire. Then PNT the two beads in Row 19. See Fig. 9. PNT the six squash beads, ear wire, and two black beads one more time. Pull tight and tie a knot. Weave excess thread back through work to hide. Cut thread.

To make the fringe, thread needle with 4'–5' of thread. String twenty-five green beads and one green drop bead. Place in the center of the thread. Then PNBT the twenty-five green beads. See Fig. 10. PNT bead on Row 19. Then PNBT twenty-five green beads and green drop bead and back up through the twenty-five beads again. Tie a knot at the top of

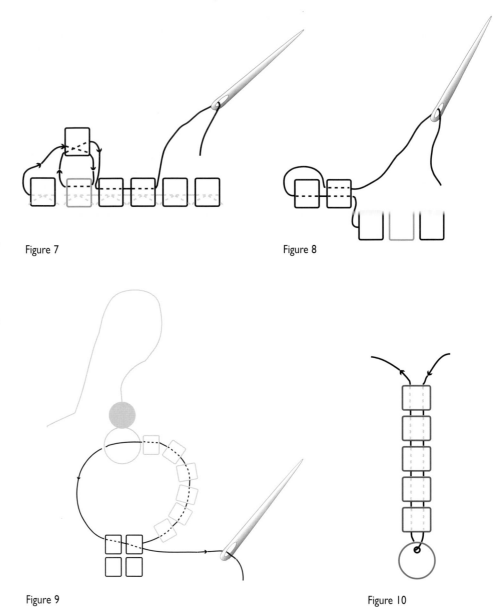

Figure 7

Figure 8

Figure 9

Figure 10

the fringe. Don't cut the excess thread. Use it to make the other two strands of fringe. To make the next fringe, string twenty-nine sapphire beads and one green drop bead, and then PNBT twenty-nine sapphire beads. See Fig. 10. Bring thread through circle of beads at the top and repeat. Tie a knot above the sapphire beads. Take the excess thread and go back down through beads to hide thread. Cut thread. To make last fringe, thread needle with other side of thread and string on twenty-nine

sapphire beads and one green drop bead. Go back up through the twenty-nine sapphire beads and bring thread through circle of beads on the opposite side of the green fringe. Go back down through sapphire beads again and come back up. Tie a knot at the top of the strand and hide end of thread in the beads. Cut.

Repeat these steps for the second earring. Remember to place fringe and earring wire on the opposite side of the fish.

Sea Turtle Bookmark

Ellen Talbott

This sea turtle bookmark was inspired by the frothy waves found in some oriental artwork and by my love of turtles and books.

The finished piece measures 7" x 2" including fringe with a 6" tail and the dragonfly charm.

MATERIALS

10 grams Japanese tubular beads, lined crystal/yellow luster, Delica #233

2 grams Japanese tubular beads, blue iris, Delica #002

7 grams Japanese tubular beads, lined crystal/green aqua luster, Delica #238

7 grams Japanese tubular beads, semi-matte silver-lined medium blue, Delica #693

4 grams Japanese tubular beads, lined green/lime, Delica #027

2 grams Japanese tubular beads, lined topaz AB, Delica #065

2 beads Japanese tubular beads, black, Delica #010

2 grams Japanese tubular beads, dyed opaque turquoise green, Delica #658

4 grams Japanese tubular beads, dyed matte transparent Kelly green, Delica #776

4 grams Japanese tubular beads, dyed opaque jade green, Delica #656

2 grams Japanese tubular beads, silver-lined smoked topaz, Delica #612

2 grams Japanese tubular beads, lined topaz/olive, Delica #273

One royal blue seed bead, size 6°

One 1/2" transparent oblong green crystal bead

One dragonfly charm

Black nylon beading thread, size D

One beading needle long, size 12

Loom

Scissors

Pliers (optional)

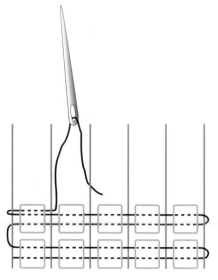

Figure 1

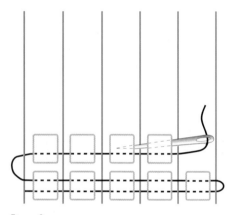

Figure 2

Warp the loom with thirty-four 40" long warp threads. Follow the design chart for fifty-five rows. Read the chart from bottom to top and right to left. For the next row, decrease one bead at each end. To decrease in loom work: after PNT last bead on the row before you wish to decrease, pass the weft thread under the outermost warp thread and PNBT the last bead. See Fig. 1. After pulling thread tight, make sure needle and thread are at the back of the work. String beads for the next row. Push the beads up into the spaces between the warp threads as usual and PNBT the beads above the warp threads, skipping the outermost warp thread on the right. See Fig. 2. Decrease one bead at each end of a row, following the design chart to the end.

Remove from loom and thread two warp threads from the center top onto the needle. String 4" of green aqua beads and tie a knot to hold beads in place. See Fig. 3.

Thread the next two warp threads onto a needle, string 4" of medium blue beads, and tie a knot to hold beads in place. Take the next two warp threads from the opposite side of the strand of green aqua beads and thread onto a needle. String 4" of yellow luster beads and tie a knot. See Fig. 4. Braid the three strands together. Tie the strands together with a knot at the top. String the 1/2" green bead and the size 6 blue seed bead onto all six threads. Bring the threads back through the green bead and tie another knot at the bottom of the bead. See Fig. 5. Weave excess thread through the strands of beads and cut. Weave the remaining warp threads at the top of the bookmark back into the beads in the body of the work.

Use the warp threads at the bottom of the bookmark to create the fringe. Follow the fringe chart and refer to the instructions on making fringe in the finishing loom bead weaving (see p. 20–22).

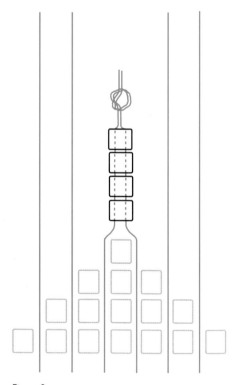

Figure 3

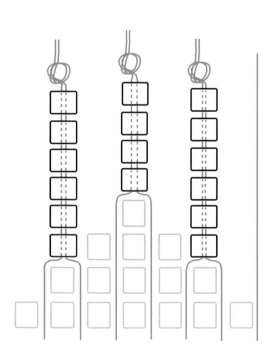

Figure 4

Figure 5

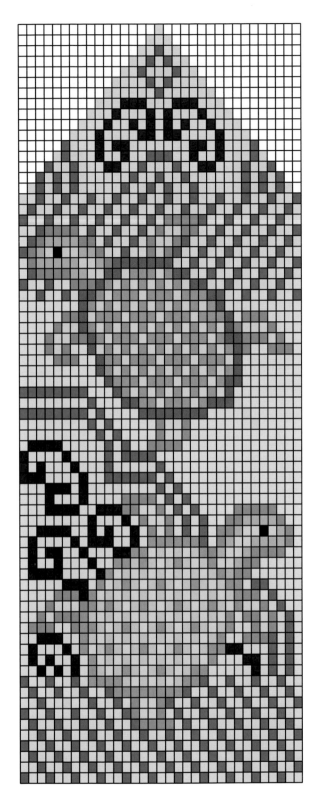

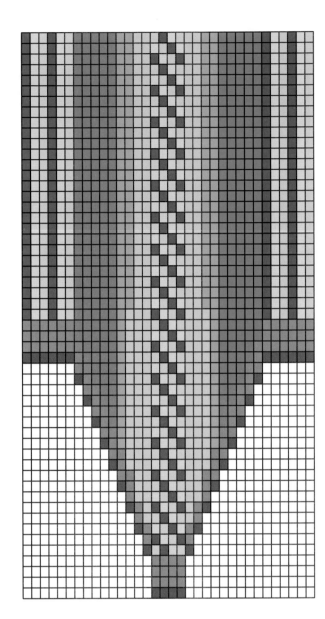

Lined crystal/yellow luster

Lined crystal/green aqua luster

Semi-matte silver-lined medium blue

Dyed matte transparent Kelly green

Dyed opaque jade green

Lined green/lime

Lined topaz

Silver-lined smoked topaz

Fringe Chart

Lined crystal/yellow luster

Semi-matte silver-lined medium blue

Blue iris

Lined crystal/green aqua luster

Dyed matte transparent Kelly green

Dyed opaque jade green

Lined green/lime

Lined topaz/olive

Silver-lined smoked topaz

Lined topaz

Dyed opaque turquoise green

Black

Design Chart

Day and Night Clock

Ellen Talbott

Worked on the loom, this fancy clock will help you keep the time day or night.

The finished piece measures 4¹/₂" x 4¹/₂".

MATERIALS

12 grams Japanese tubular beads, blue iris, Delica #002

10 grams Japanese tubular beads, silver-lined sapphire, Delica #047

10 grams Japanese tubular beads, Ceylon light yellow, Delica #203

7 grams Japanese tubular beads, opaque yellow AB, Delica #160

4 grams Japanese tubular beads, semi-matte silver-lined squash, Delica #681

4 grams Japanese tubular beads, semi-matte silver-lined orange, Delica #682

4 grams Japanese tubular beads, semi-matte silver-lined dark ruby, Delica #683

4 grams Japanese tubular beads, transparent gray iris, Delica #107

4 grams Japanese tubular beads, matte cream, Delica #352

2 grams Japanese tubular beads, white pearl, Delica #201

2 grams Japanese tubular beads, opaque black, Delica #010

Twelve Japanese tubular beads, transparent gray olive luster, Delica #123

Four Japanese tubular beads, dyed opaque turquoise green, Delica #658

Black nylon beading thread, size D

Two long beading needles, size 12

Loom (wide enough to hold eighty warp threads)

Clock movement for a 3/4" thick clock face with white hour and minute hands

3/4" thick unfinished pine clock face (7" x 7")

Black gloss acrylic paint

Small paintbrush

Glue

Reverse these instructions if you are left-handed.

Warp the loom with eighty warp threads at least 17" long. Thread the needle and attach this weft thread to the outer left warp thread with an overhand knot, leaving a tail about 6" long. String on all the beads in the first row according to the design chart. Read the chart from left to right and from bottom to top. Make sure to count your beads correctly, because you won't know if you've made a mistake until you have finished the row. Because of the width of the design, you will have to PNT the beads in stages. Starting at the right edge, push up seven or eight beads at a time and PNT. Continue in this manner to the end of the row. Work according to design chart for thirty-one rows.

To create the center hole, string on thirty-six beads according to the chart and push above the warp threads on Row 32. PNBT all thirty-

- ☐ Opaque yellow AB
- ☐ Semi-matte silver-lined squash
- ☐ Semi-matte silver-lined orange
- ■ Semi-matte silver-lined dark ruby
- ☐ Transparent gray iris
- ☐ Ceylon light yellow
- ☐ Matte cream
- ☐ White pearl
- ■ Opaque black
- ■ Silver-lined sapphire
- ■ Blue iris
- ☐ Transparent gray olive luster
- ■ Dyed opaque turquoise green

Design Chart

six beads above the warp threads. Then thread the other needle with a new weft thread. Weave the thread up through the body of the work to anchor it. Skipping the seven middle spaces between the warp threads, make sure the needle comes out of the thirty-sixth bead from the right edge. Take the needle to the back of the work and PNBT all thirty-six beads. See Fig. 1. Do five more rows, working each side separately and leaving the seven center spaces in the warp threads empty.

For the next row, abandon the needle on the right side. Weave in excess thread later. Using the needle on the left side, continue to follow the design chart, filling in all spaces between the warp threads.

Weave the next thirty rows according to the design chart.

To end, weave several rows without beads to create a thread cloth on both ends. Remove from the loom and tie off warp threads using the

surgeon's knot. Trim thread ends, fold over thread cloth to the back of the work, and glue in place.

Now you are ready to prepare the pine clock face. Sand the wood, if necessary, and paint two or three coats of black gloss acrylic paint. Let the paint dry. Next, glue the beads to the wooden base. Line up the hole in the wood with the hole in the beadwork. Make sure the edges are straight and even. Put a few books on top to hold the beads in place while the glue dries. To allow for the

width of the beads, remove the rubber cushion that comes in the clock movement assembly. Push the shaft of the clock up through the hole in the wood and between the warp threads. Carefully separate the warp threads and push them off to the side as you bring the shaft up between them. Follow the instructions that come with the clock movement to assemble the hands. If you can't find white hands, paint them white before you assemble them.

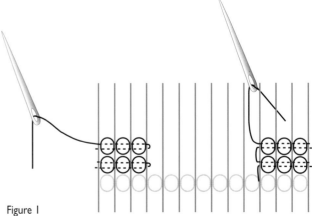

Figure I

Egyptian Column Bracelet

Ellen Talbott

Inspired by ancient Egyptian columns, this loomed bracelet will take you back to the time of the Pharaohs.

The finished piece measures 7¹/₂" x ³/₄".

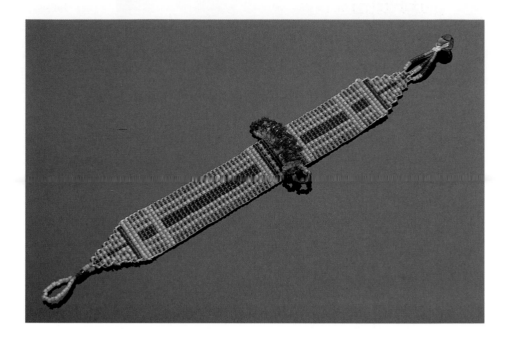

MATERIALS

2 grams Japanese tubular beads, transparent dark tangerine, Delica #704

2 grams Japanese tubular beads, matte light blue, Delica #862

2 grams Japanese tubular beads, dyed opaque squash, Delica #651

One ³/₈" oval amber bead

White nylon beading thread, size D

One beading needle, size 10

Loom

Scissors

Warp the loom with fourteen 19" long warp threads. The first eleven rows will be worked later. Be sure to leave enough room, about 1", on the warp threads for these eleven rows before you start. Starting with Row 12 on the design chart, follow the chart for the next thirty-eight rows. Read the chart from left to right and from bottom to top.

The next row is the loop row. For this row, string on four squash beads, *one blue bead, five tangerine beads, one blue bead, nine squash beads.* Repeat between asterisks eleven times. Then string on one blue bead, five tangerine beads, one blue bead, and five squash beads.

Working from right to left, push up the last bead into the first space created by the first and second warp threads and PNT bead to hold it in place. The loops will be formed at the back of the work. Go to the next fifth squash bead, push it up through the second space between warp threads, and PNT the bead. Continue in this manner until the end of the row. This work is awkward, but it will be over soon.

Work the next twenty-five rows on the design chart. On the next row, you will be decreasing one bead on each side. To decrease: after PNT the last bead on the row before you want to decrease, pass the weft thread under the outermost warp thread and go back through the last bead. See Fig. 1. After pulling the thread tight, make sure the needle and thread are at the back of the work. String the beads for the decreased

row. Push the beads up into the spaces between the warp threads as usual and PNBT the beads above the warp threads, skipping the outermost warp thread. See Fig. 2. Decrease according to chart for the next ten rows.

Remove needle from the thread, get a new strand of thread, and thread the needle. Turn the loom around and weave thread into the body of the work to anchor it. Make sure the needle is coming out on the first row worked on the left. Weave the first eleven rows following the chart from Row 11 to Row 1 and decrease as shown in Figs. 1 and 2 to create the other end of the bracelet. Weave excess thread into the body of work and cut. Remove from the loom.

Now you are ready to create the button and loop closure. Begin with one end of the bracelet and weave in the warp threads, except for the center four threads. Thread the center two warp threads onto a needle, and string two squash beads and three tangerine beads; leave for now. Thread the warp thread to one side

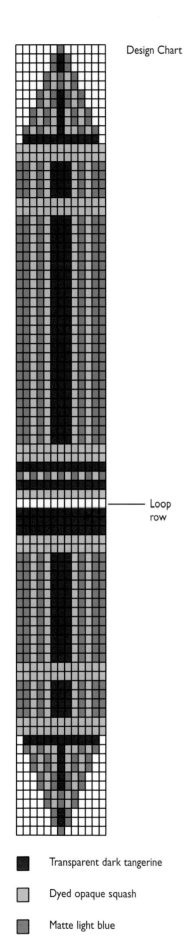

Design Chart

Loop row

■ Transparent dark tangerine

□ Dyed opaque squash

▨ Matte light blue

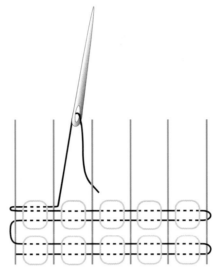

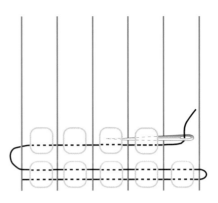

Figure 1

Figure 2

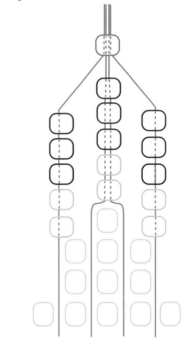

Figure 3

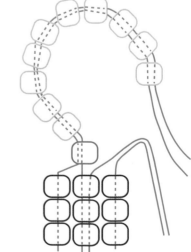

Figure 4

of the center strand onto a needle and string three squash beads and three tangerine beads. Repeat with opposite warp thread. String one blue bead onto all four threads. See Fig. 3. Next, string twenty-two squash beads (or enough to fit over the amber bead) onto the two warp threads on the left. Take the other two threads and PNT the twenty-two squash beads in the opposite direction. See Fig. 4. Pull tight and tie a knot below the loop of beads. Hide the excess thread ends in the beads and cut.

Now begin work on the other end of the bracelet. Weave in the warp threads, leaving the center four threads. Thread the center two warp threads onto a needle and string three squash beads, five tangerine beads, and one blue bead; leave for now. Thread warp thread to one side of the center strand onto a needle and string three squash beads, five tangerine beads, and three blue beads. Repeat with opposite warp thread. Tie an overhand knot, using all four warp threads to secure beads. Thread all four warp threads through the amber bead and tie another knot under the bead. Weave excess thread back up through beads to hide ends.

Water Lily Comb

Ellen Talbott

This quick-and-easy loom project matches the Water Lily Mirror (see p. 117).

The finished piece measures 8" x 1¼".

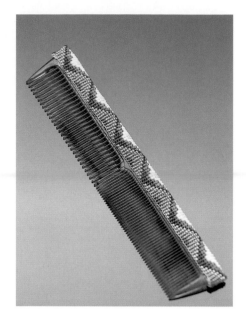

MATERIALS

Three hundred and twelve transparent silver-lined royal blue seed beads, size 11°

Three hundred and twelve metallic light green seed beads, size 11°

Two hundred and eighty-eight transparent iridescent light green seed beads, size 11°

Two hundred and sixty-four opaque white seed beads, size 11°

Two hundred and forty turquoise white heart seed beads, size 11°

Seventy-two transparent forest-green seed beads, size 11°

Forty-eight iridescent opaque yellow seed beads, size 11°

White nylon beading thread, size D

One beading needle, size 12

8" comb (one that has square ends)

Scissors

Glue

Warp your loom with seventeen warp threads, 20" long. Read the design chart from left to right and from bottom to top. If you are left-handed, read the chart from right to left. Attach the weft thread to left outermost warp thread (reverse, if left handed) and weave according to design chart for ninety-six rows. End the work by weaving ten or more rows of thread cloth to the top of the work. When you are done with this end, turn the loom around and create a bit of thread cloth at the other end. This keeps the beads from moving along the warp threads and falling off. Remove from the loom and tie off all pairs of warp threads with surgeon's knots. Trim the ends and fold thread cloth to the back of the work and glue in place. Next, glue work to the spine of the comb. Make sure that the design is lined up evenly along the spine. If necessary, temporarily sew the beadwork onto the comb to hold it in place while the glue dries. To sew it in place, catch the outer warp threads with your needle and take the thread back and forth between the teeth of the comb. Before the glue dries, sew the work together at both ends of the comb. After the glue dries, cut and remove the thread used to hold the beading in place.

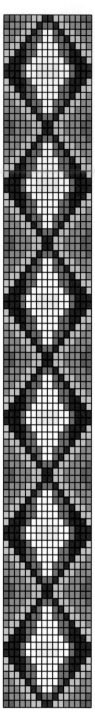

Design Chart

■ Transparent silver-lined royal blue

■ Turquoise white heart

■ Transparent forest green

■ Transparent iridescent light green

□ Metallic light green

□ Iridescent opaque yellow

□ Opaque white

Tri-Diamond Headband

Ellen Talbott

This colorful headband is a good loom project for a beginner.

The finished piece measures 11¹⁄₄" x ¹⁄₂".

MATERIALS

Four hundred and forty-eight transparent silver-lined royal blue seed beads, size 11°

Three hundred and six turquoise white heart seed beads, size 11°

Two hundred and ten opaque white seed beads, size 11°

One hundred and eighty-four metallic light green seed beads, size 11°

Twenty-nine iridescent opaque yellow seed beads, size 11°

White nylon beading thread, size D

One beading needle, size 12

¹⁄₂" plastic headband

Loom

Scissors

Glue

Warp the loom with ten 24" long warp threads. Read the design chart from left to right and from bottom to top. If you're left-handed, read the chart from right to left. Attach weft thread to the left outermost warp thread (reverse if left-handed) and weave according to the design chart for 131 rows. End by weaving ten or more rows of thread cloth to the top of the work. When you are done with this end, turn the loom around and create a bit of thread cloth at the other end. This keeps the beads from moving along the warp threads and falling off. Remove from the loom and tie off all pairs of warp threads with surgeon's knots. Trim the ends and fold the warp cloth to the back of the work and glue in place.

Glue finished beadwork to the headband. Align the center diamond with the center of the headband. If necessary, temporarily sew the beadwork in place by catching the outermost warp threads every ¹⁄₂" or so on either side, taking the thread back and forth underneath the headband. When the glue is dry, cut and remove the thread used to hold the beadwork in place.

Design Chart

☐ Opaque white

☐ Iridescent opaque yellow

▨ Metallic light green

▨ Turquoise white heart

■ Transparent silver-lined royal blue

Parakeet Paradise Wall Hanging

Ellen Talbott

Inspired by a lithograph by H.C. Richter (1821–1902), these colorful birds will brighten up any room.

The finished piece measures 7¹/₂" x 3³/₄".

MATERIALS

1¹/₂ oz transparent iridescent gold seed beads, size 11°

¹/₂ oz opaque iridescent yellow seed beads, size 11°

¹/₂ oz opaque light blue seed beads, size 11°

¹/₂ oz silver-lined transparent royal blue seed beads, size 11°

¹/₂ oz transparent Kelly green seed beads, size 11°

¹/₂ oz silver-lined transparent dark red seed beads, size 11°

¹/₄ oz opaque light green seed beads, size 11°

¹/₄ oz opaque black seed beads, size 11°

¹/₄ oz opaque light orange seed beads, size 11°

¹/₄ oz opaque brown seed beads, size 11°

¹/₄ oz opaque dark brown seed beads, size 11°

¹/₄ oz pearl white seed beads, size 11°

¹/₄ oz transparent off-white seed beads, size 11°

¹/₄ oz transparent forest green seed beads, size 11°

¹/₄ oz silver-lined transparent green seed beads, size 11°

¹/₄ oz transparent dark green seed beads, size 11°

One beading needle, size 12

White nylon beading thread, size D

Loom (wide enough for sixty-three warp threads)

Scissors

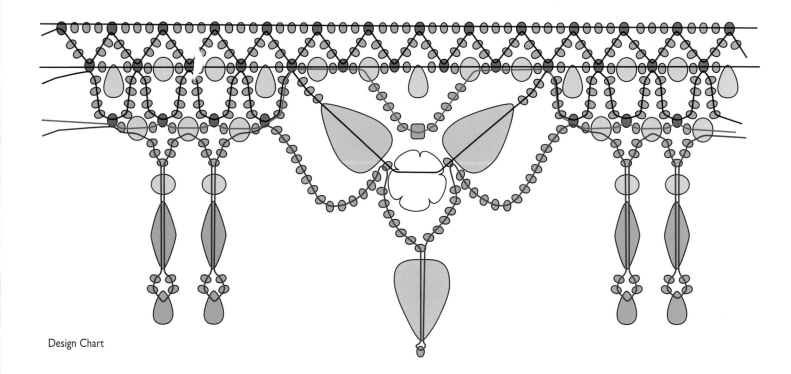

Design Chart

ROUND 3: *String one size 11° matte, one size 6°, one size 11° matte. PNT the next size 8° on Round 2. Repeat once. String one size 11° matte, one turquoise drop, one size 11° matte. PNT the next size 8° bead on Round 2.* Repeat between asterisks eight times.

ROUND 4: *String three size 11° matte, one leaf, one size 11° matte, one flower, one size 11° matte, one leaf, and three size 11° matte. PNT the fifth size 8° bead. String four size 11° sea green, one size 8°, and four size 11° sea green. PNT the next size 8° bead. Repeat three times.* Repeat between asterisks two more times.

ROUND 5: PNT the next six beads on Round 3, coming out a size 6°. **String five size 11° sea green, one small square, and five size 11° sea green. PNT the next size 6° bead and the next six beads on Round 3, coming out a size 8°. PNT the four size 11° sea green and one size 8° from Round 4. *String one size 11° sea green, one size 6°, and one size 11° sea green. PNT the next size 8° in Round 4.* Repeat between asterisks two more times. PNT the next four size 11° sea green in Round 4 and the next seven beads in Round 3, coming out a size 6°.** Repeat between double asterisks once more, and then once again, except for the last two sentences.

ROUND 6: **String fourteen size 11° sea green. PNT the size 11° matte between the leaf and flower. String seven size 11° sea green, one leaf, and one size 11° sea green. PNBT the leaf and one size 11° sea green. String six size 11° sea green. PNT the next size 11° matte between the flower and leaf. String thirteen size 11° sea green. PNT the next size 8° bead in Round 4 and the size 11° and size 6° in Round 5. *String three size 11° sea green, one size 6°, one bi-cone, two size 11° sea green, one sea green drop, and two size 11° sea green. PNBT the bi-cone size 6° and one size 11° sea green. String two size 11° sea green and PNT the next size 6° bead on Round 5.* Repeat between asterisks. PNT the next two beads, coming out a size 8° on Round 4.** Repeat between double asterisks twice more. Tie off and weave in ends.

Netted Christmas Ornament

Jane Davis

This is a quick project that can be adapted to any shape of ball with a little experimentation. The middle and bottom fringe can make a big difference in the look of the ornament. Use cream colors and hang shells for a beach theme, or gold and silver with large Swarovski crystals for a glittery look. But most of all, have fun!

The samples shown were beaded on hand-blown, egg-shaped ornaments approximately 1³/₄" x 2¹/₄". Instructions follow for the ornament in the vibrant Christmas colors on the right. To use a 2¹/₄" round glass ball, use size 11° seed beads instead of the Delicas, and follow the basic instructions after making the adjustments listed at the end of the project.

MATERIALS

4 grams Japanese tubular beads, silver-lined red, Delica #602
5 grams Japanese tubular beads, silver-lined emerald, Delica #605
1 gram Japanese tubular beads, silver-lined gold, Delica #42
2 grams Japanese tubular beads, silver-lined violet, Delica #610
1³/₄" x 2¹/₂" glass ball or 2¹/₄" round glass ball
Six red center-drilled glass disks
Twelve ¹/₂" bugle beads
Six ³/₈" long by ¹/₈" thick bugle beads
Eighteen 3mm round red glass beads
Beading thread, size B
Beading needle, size 12
Scissors

For the first six rounds, work the netting in a flat circle on a table. On Round 7, place your beading on the glass ball. On Rounds 7, 9 13, and 16 (decrease rounds), adjust the netting by pulling it tightly down so that it clings to the ball and the beads in the decrease round do not have gaps of thread.

ROUND 1: String twelve repeats of three violet beads and one gold bead. Tie the tail end and working thread into a square knot to form a circle, leaving a 6" tail to knot and weave into the netting.

ROUND 2: Position the circle so that the thread is coming out the right side of a gold bead. String three violet, one gold, three violet. PNT the next gold bead on Round 1. Repeat all around the circle. PNT the first three violet beads and the first gold bead in the round.

ROUNDS 3–4: Following the design chart, complete Rounds 3 and 4 in the same manner as Round 2, using three red, one gold, and three red for Round 3, and four green, one gold, and four green for Round 4.

ROUND 5: Complete Round 5 the same as the previous rounds, using five green, one gold, and five green beads around. However, at the end of the round, instead of passing

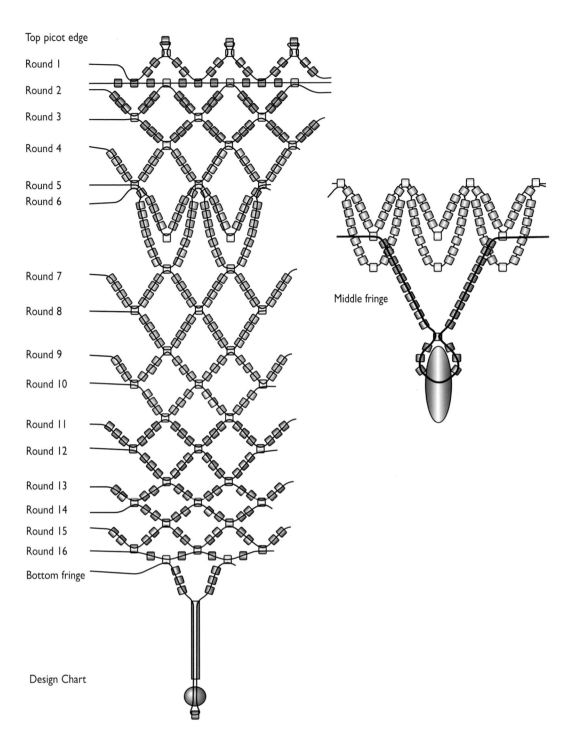

Top picot edge

Round 1

Round 2

Round 3

Round 4

Round 5
Round 6

Round 7

Round 8

Round 9

Round 10

Round 11

Round 12

Round 13

Round 14

Round 15

Round 16

Bottom fringe

Design Chart

Middle fringe

through the first five green and one gold bead to prepare for the next round, only PNT the first green bead strung at the beginning of the round. Now you are ready for Round 6.

ROUND 6: String seven green, one gold, seven green beads, and PNT one green, one gold, and one green bead. Repeat around. At the end of the round, PNT the first seven beads in the round and one gold bead.

ROUNDS 7–15: Following the design chart, complete these rounds the same as Round 2 using the appropriate number and color of beads.

ROUND 16: String one red, one gold, one red, and PNT the next green bead. Repeat around, then string through the whole round again. Tighten this round by pulling the netting down snugly around the ball. PNT one red and one gold bead.

BOTTOM FRINGE ROUND: String three red, one bugle, one 3mm round, one violet Delica. Skip the violet Delica and PNBT the 3mm round and bugle bead. String three red Delicas and PNT the next gold bead on Round 16. Repeat around.

MIDDLE FRINGE: Begin a new thread or PNBT the beads up to Round 5. PNT the beads on a section of Round 5 so that the needle is coming out the left side of a gold bead as shown on the middle fringe round of the design chart. String fourteen red Delicas, one disk, three red Delicas. PNT the fourth Delica on the other side of the disk. String ten red Delicas. Skip the second hanging gold bead on Round 5 and PNT the third hanging gold bead on Round 5. Repeat five times. PNT the beads on Round 5 so that the thread is coming out the next hanging gold bead. String twelve red Delicas, one 1/8" thick bugle bead, three red Delicas, one 3mm round, three red Delicas. PNBT the bugle bead. String twelve

red Delicas. Pass the needle under the strand of beads with the disk and through the gold bead. Repeat around. PNUT the beads to Round 1.

TOP PICOT EDGE: Position the thread so that it is coming out of the middle violet bead in one of the Round 1 sections. String two red, one gold, one violet, and PNBT the gold. String two red and PNT the next middle violet bead on Round 1. Repeat this sequence around the top of the ornament, alternating a green bead and a violet bead for the tip of the picot. Tie off and weave in thread.

ADJUSTMENT FOR A 2¼" ROUND GLASS BALL:
Rounds 7–9 have five beads, one bead, and five beads in each repeat.

The next four rounds have four beads, one bead, and four beads in each repeat.

The next round has three beads, one bead, and three beads in each repeat.

The next two rounds have two beads, one bead, and two beads in each repeat.

The last round, bottom and middle fringe, and top picot edge are the same as the listed instructions.

Angel Christmas Ornament

Jane Davis

If you or someone you love collects angels, this is the perfect holiday project to make for the Christmas tree.

The finished piece measures 2¹/₂" × 3³/₄".

MATERIALS

- 8" 20-gauge wire (for wings and hanger)
- 4" 24-gauge wire (for halo, head, and neck)
- Thirty frosted white seed beads, size 6° (for wings and dress)
- ¹/₄ oz clear iridescent seed beads, size 11° (for wings and dress)
- Thirty ⁵/₈"-long bugle beads, frosted white (for wings and body)
- 4 grams Japanese tubular beads,

white opal, Delicas #220 (for wings, body, and dress)
- 2 grams Japanese tubular beads, silver-lined crystal, Delicas #41 (for dress)
- Six ¹/₄"-long pearl bugle beads, or niblets (for wings)
- Eight three-sided beads, frosted very light pink or white egglet beads (for wings)
- Three rose quartz 4mm round beads

(for neck and hands)
- One rose quartz disk (for head)
- One star (for accent)
- Four ¹/₄" bugle beads, or niblets, frosted white (for arms)
- Beading thread of your choice
- Beading needle, size 12 or 10
- Scissors
- Roundnose pliers
- Flat nose pliers (optional)
- Wire cutters

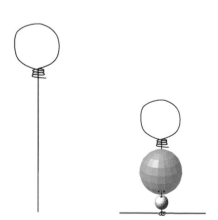

Figure 1   Figure 2

■ Head and Wings

Cut 2" off the 8" length of 20-gauge wire (this will become the hanger). Make a halo at one end of the 4" 24-gauge wire by looping the wire around your finger. Then neatly wind the end around the wire two times and cut any excess. See Fig. 1.

String the quartz disk and one quartz 4mm round. Wrap the remaining end of the wire neatly

around the center of the 20-gauge wire. See Fig. 2.

Bend the 20-gauge wire until it follows the same shape as Fig. 3. String nineteen beads onto one side of the 20-gauge wire. Check to make sure that the angel head is in the middle of the 20-gauge wire. Cut the beaded end of the 20-gauge wire to about ³/₁₆" from the last bead and roll it into a loop with roundnose pliers to hold the beads in place. Repeat for the other wing.

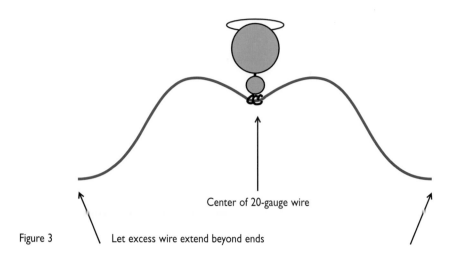

Figure 3

Center of 20-gauge wire

Let excess wire extend beyond ends

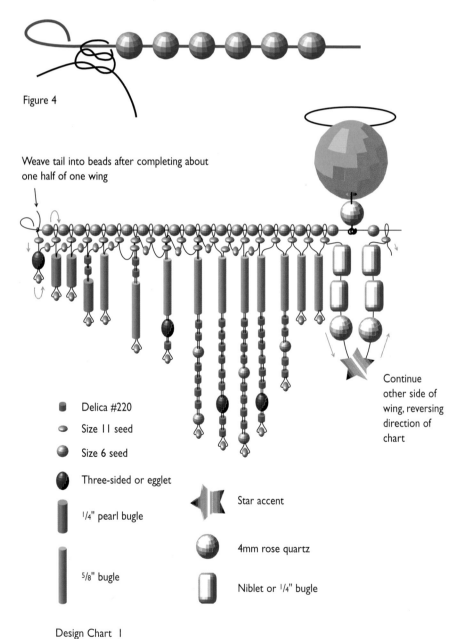

Figure 4

Weave tail into beads after completing about one half of one wing

Continue other side of wing, reversing direction of chart

- Delica #220
- Size 11 seed
- Size 6 seed
- Three-sided or egglet
- ¼" pearl bugle
- ⅝" bugle
- Star accent
- 4mm rose quartz
- Niblet or ¼" bugle

Design Chart 1

Begin the wing fringe by tying a 9' length of beading thread into a square knot on the end of the 20-gauge wire between the loop and the last bead. See Fig. 4. Following Design Chart 1, string the beads as indicated, then pass the needle back up through the beads and over the 20-gauge wire between the size 6 beads. Continue across one wing, then make the angel's arms and the other wing by following the chart in reverse.

Set this part aside to make the netted angel body.

■ **Angel Body**

Step 1: Using a 9' beading thread, string one bugle bead, one Delica, one bugle, and one Delica. Tie the tail end and working end of threads into a square knot, leaving a 1' tail. This will be used to attach the body to the wings. String through the first three beads again. See Fig. 5. Step 2: String one Delica, one bugle bead, and one Delica. PNT the third, fifth, and sixth beads again. See Fig. 6.

Step 3: String one Delica, one bugle bead, and one Delica. PNT the sixth, eighth, and ninth beads again. See Fig. 7.

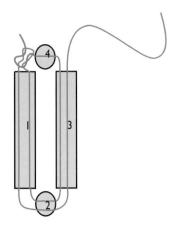

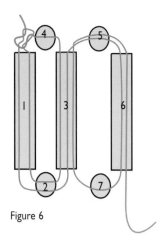

Figure 5

Figure 6

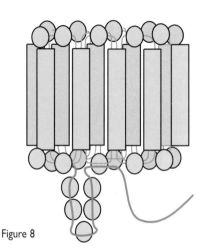

Figure 7

Repeat the sequence of Steps 2 and 3 until there are ten bugle beads. String one Delica and PNT the first bugle bead. String one Delica and PNT the tenth bugle bead.

PNBT the Delica so that the tail thread and the working thread meet. Tie a square knot. PNBT the bugle bead and one Delica. The tail thread is now at one end of the tube of beads, ready to attach to the angel wings, and the working thread is on the other end, ready to begin netting on the angel dress.

■ Angel Dress

The first three rounds are easier if you slip the body onto a pencil or dowel. Be careful at this point and make sure you don't skip any Delicas on the body. Because they are gathered and all bunched up, it's a good idea to count the number of loops made after each of the first three rounds to make sure there are ten loops in each round.

ROUND 1: String two white Delicas, one silver Delica, two white Delicas, and PNT the next Delica on the body. See Fig. 8. Repeat around the body. PNBT the first three beads again.

ROUNDS 2–7: Continue as for Round 1, following Design Chart 2 for the number of beads in each round.

ROUND 8: String four Delicas, one size 11°, one size 6°, one size 11°, four Delicas, and PNT the next silver Delica in Round 7. String two Delicas, one size 11°, one size 6°, one size 11°, two Delicas, and PNBT the same silver Delica on Round 7. See

Figure 8

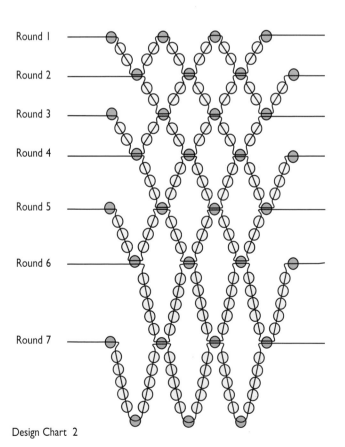

Round 1

Round 2

Round 3

Round 4

Round 5

Round 6

Round 7

Design Chart 2

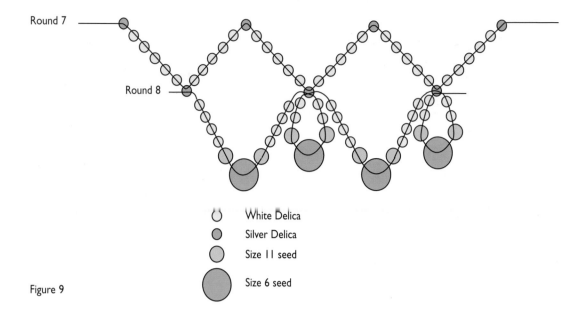

Round 7

Round 8

○ White Delica

● Silver Delica

○ Size 11 seed

● Size 6 seed

Figure 9

Fig. 9. Repeat around bottom of dress. Tie off and hide working thread.

■ Attaching Body to Wings

To stitch the body to the wings, PNT a Delica at the top of the body, string a size 11° seed bead, and wrap the thread over the wire of the wings, then back through the seed bead and the next Delica on the body. Repeat across one side of the body, then across the other side, but PNT the size 11° seed beads already strung so that the body is stitched together at the top. Tie off and hide thread.

■ Hanger

Make a loop in one end of the 2" length of 20-gauge wire and close at base of halo. Make a small loop at the other end of the 20-gauge wire and bend into a hanger shape.

4

PRE-STRUNG
BEAD
PROJECTS

Envelope Jewelry Case

Jane Davis

Pamper your favorite necklace with this elegant jewelry case, lined in ultra suede. For those who love to knit, this is a good transition project for grasping the basics of bead knitting.

The finished piece measures 4³/₄" x 3³/₄" when closed.

Detail of Envelope Jewelry Case

MATERIALS

KNITTING SUPPLIES

2¹/₄ oz or 60 grams background color seed beads, size 8°

¹/₄ oz or 6 grams pale green seed beads, size 8°

¹/₈ oz or 3 grams pale pink seed beads, size 8°

¹/₈ oz or 3 grams pale lavender seed beads, size 8°

¹/₄ oz or 4 grams pink seed beads, size 8°

Knitting needles, size 0

Beading needle, size 10

One twisted wire beading needle

Cotton Cord (one of the following types in a color that blends with your background bead color):

Two balls DMC Cebelia, size 10 (use as doubled throughout work)

or

One ball Mondial Cotone "Marea 5"

or

One 50-gram ball Coats Opera 5

A basket, bowl, or other container to hold your ball of cotton when moving beads down the cord.

Paper and paper scissors for cutting dividers between rows

Crochet hook to help correct errors

FINISHING SUPPLIES

¹/₂ oz or 14 grams size 11° seed beads to match background bead color

Twenty fringe beads

¹/₄ yard ultra suede or pig suede (Measure your knitting before purchase to make sure the size is correct. The suede needs to be the same size as your knitting.)

¹/₄ yard woven fusible interfacing

Sew-on snap, size 3

Nylon beading thread, size B, or quilting thread to match seed beads

Sewing needles

Thimble

Scissors

■ Abbreviations

KB: Knit bead

PB: Purl bead

K2tog: Knit 2 stitches together

P2tog: Purl 2 stitches together

Sl 1, K1, psso: Slip a stitch from the left needle to the right needle as if to knit but without working it, knit the next stitch, pass the slipped stitch over the knit stitch and off the right needle.

Sl 1, P1, psso: Slip a stitch from the left needle to the right needle as if to purl without working it, purl the next stitch, pass the slipped stitch over the purl stitch and off the right needle.

On Design Chart 1, beginning at Row 33, string size 8 beads and work down to Row 2, from either left to right or right to left (the design is symmetrical) onto the cotton cord. At the end of each row, string on a small piece of paper (about 3/8" square). This helps keep track of the rows. It is torn off as you get to it while knitting.

On size 0 needles, cast on thirty-nine stitches (simple cast on).

ROW 1: Purl

ROW 2: K2, KB36, K1

ROW 3: P1, PB37, P1

Repeat Row 2 for all even rows through Row 32.

Repeat Row 3 for all odd rows through Row 33.

Cut the cord leaving a 6" tail. On Design Chart 2, beginning at Row 95, string size 8 beads and work down to Row 34 in the same manner as before.

Tie cord onto knitting at Row 33, and continue knitting odd and even rows as before through Row 68.

ROW 69: P2, PB35, P2

ROW 70: Sl 1, K1, psso, K1, KB34, K2

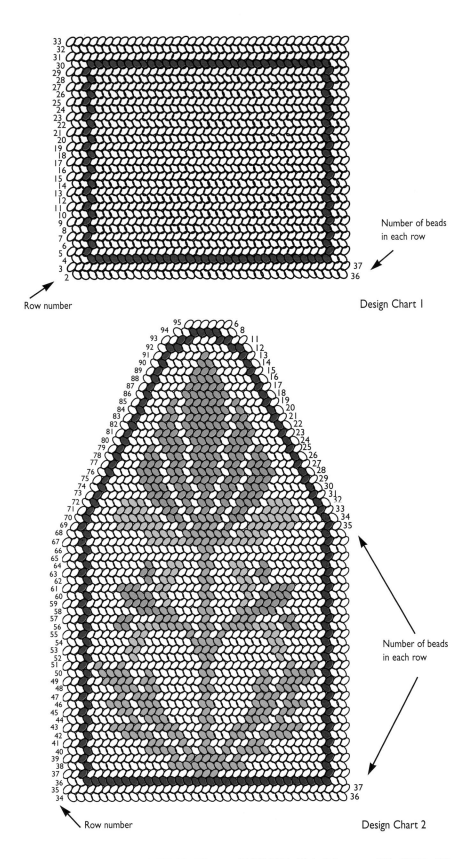

Number of beads in each row

Design Chart 1

Row number

Number of beads in each row

Design Chart 2

Row number

ROW 71: Sl 1, P1, psso, P1, PB33, P2

ROW 72: Sl 1, K1, psso, K1, KB32, K2

ROW 73: Sl 1, P1, psso, P1, PB31, P2

ROW 74: Sl 1, K1, psso, K1, KB30, K2

ROW 75: Sl 1, P1, psso, P1, PB29, P2

ROW 76: Sl 1, K1, psso, K1, KB28, K2

ROW 77: Sl 1, P1, psso, P1, PB27, P2

ROW 78: Sl 1, K1, psso, K1, KB26, K2

ROW 79: Sl 1, P1, psso, P1, PB25, P2

ROW 80: Sl 1, K1, psso, K1, KB24, K2

ROW 81: Sl 1, P1, psso, P1, PB23, P2

ROW 82: Sl 1, K1, psso, K1, KB22, K2

ROW 83: Sl 1, P1, psso, P1, PB21, P2

ROW 84: Sl 1, K1, psso, K1, KB20, K2

ROW 85: Sl 1, P1, psso, P1, PB19, P2

ROW 86: Sl 1, K1, psso, K1, KB18, K2

ROW 87: Sl 1, P1, psso, P1, PB17, P2

ROW 88: Sl 1, K1, psso, K1, KB16, K2

ROW 89: Sl 1, P1, psso, P1, PB15, P2

ROW 90: Sl 1, K1, psso, K1, KB14, K2

ROW 91: Sl 1, P1, psso, P1, PB13, P2

ROW 92: Sl 1, K1, psso, K1, KB12, K2

ROW 93: Sl 1, P1, psso, P1, PB11, P2

ROW 94: Sl 1, K1, psso, K2, KB8, K3

ROW 95: Sl 1, P1, psso, P2, PB6, P2, P2tog

ROW 96: Sl 1, K1, psso, K8, K2tog

Cast off in purl.

■ Blocking

Hold the knitted piece under the faucet until it is wet through. Blot out excess water with a dishcloth. Check that all the beads are on the front of the piece and adjust any as needed. Lay the piece right side up on a cookie sheet and carefully flatten and straighten the piece, making sure all the selvedge edges are not turned under. Turn on your oven to 200°, then turn it off after it has warmed up. Leave the cookie sheet in the oven overnight.

Sew in all loose thread tails.

■ Lining

Lay your knitted piece on top of Fig. 1 to be sure that the lining fits your piece. The lining should be about ⅛" to ¼" smaller all around. Adjust the

Figure 1

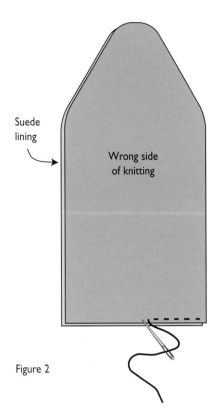

Suede lining →

Wrong side of knitting

Figure 2

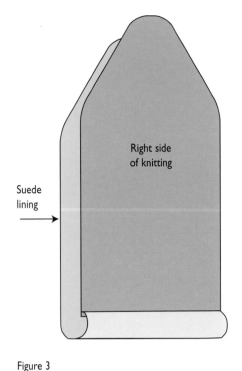

Suede lining →

Right side of knitting

Figure 3

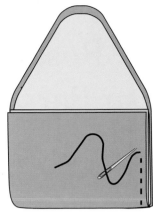

Figure 4

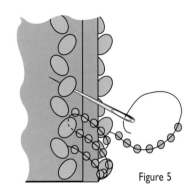

Figure 5

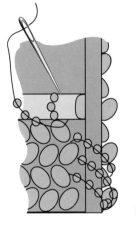

Figure 6

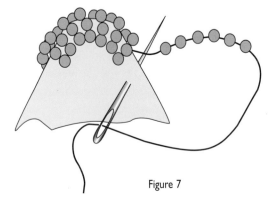

Figure 7

guide if necessary, then cut the interfacing. It should cover the back side of the beads, but not the back side of the selvedge. Iron on to the wrong side of your knitting.

Sew the female side of the snap to the front of the case centered over Row 23. Cut the ultra suede the same size as the knitting. Place the right sides of the ultra suede on the knitting together. Using a running stitch, join as close as possible to the first row of beads. See Fig. 2. Turn the ultra suede to the wrong side of the case as in Fig. 3, then fold up the bottom of the case at the fold line, smoothing out the ultra suede and lining it up with the edges of the case. Pin in place. Use a matching color thread (quilting thread or beading thread) to stitch the sides in place with a running stitch close to the first column of beads and catching the suede in each stitch. See Fig. 4.

Overcast stitch around the sides of the case by stringing seven size 11° seed beads for each stitch and passing through the size 8 beads at the edge of the knitting. See Fig. 5. At the sides of the opening, cover the raw edges of the suede by making three vertical stitches, each with three beads per stitch. See Fig. 6. Cover the edge of the knitting and the edge of the suede all along the flap with six size 11° seed beads on each stitch around the edge. See Fig. 7

Sew the fringe by passing through one size 8° bead on Row 33 of the knitting. String two size 11° seed beads, one fringe bead, and two size 11° seed beads. Then skip the next bead on the knitting and pass though the third bead on the knitting. Continue in this pattern all across Row 33, always stitching through the beads on the knitting in the same direction (i.e., either from the back to the front or the front to the back).

Sew the male side of the snap to the flap, being careful to line it up with the female side of the snap when the case is closed.

Wild Rose Clasp Purse

Jane Davis

This purse represents a small tour de force for bead knitters. It combines bead knitting and shaping, which is not commonly done. It is tedious enough just to string on the bead design and knit it up with straight sides. Keep close attention on each row to ensure that the beads line up in the proper order. For beaders who also love to knit, it is a joy to make this little treasure.

The purse and fringe measure 3¹/₂" x 5¹/₂" on a 10" chain.

MATERIALS

Knitting needles, size 0000

One hank or 2 oz or 56 grams light blue seed beads, size 11° (for background)

1¹/₂ oz or 42 grams light green seed beads, size 11° (for leaves)

1¹/₂ oz or 42 grams medium green seed beads, size 11° (for leaves)

1¹/₂ oz or 42 grams dark green seed beads, size 11° (for leaves)

1¹/₂ oz or 42 grams pale pink seed beads, size 11° (for flower petals)

1¹/₂ oz or 42 grams pink seed beads, size 11° (for flower petals)

1¹/₂ oz or 42 grams salmon-pink seed beads, size 11° (for flower petals)

1¹/₂ oz or 42 grams salmon-red seed beads, size 11° (for flower petals)

Twenty-nine purple seed beads, size 11° (for flower center)

Eighteen yellow seed beads, size 11° (for bee and flower center)

Eight black seed beads, size 11° (for bee)

Twelve light gray seed beads, size 11° (for bee's wings)

Four dark gray seed beads, size 11° (for bee's wings)

Twenty clear AB finish seed beads, size 11° (for chain)

5 grams clear AB seed beads, size 15° (for clasp lining, fringe, and chain)

One small teardrop bead (for inside clasp lining)

Fourteen small dagger drop beads (for fringe)

Twenty pale blue-lined, clear AB finish, size 8° (for chain)

Eight clear AB finish, size 6° (for chain)

Two faceted, size 5° (for chain)

Eight Japanese tubular beads, silver lined, Delica #41 (for chain)

2¹/₂" clasp

Note: You will need to use the same shaped clasp as in the photo, since this design will not fit a 2¹/₂" clasp with a dif-

ferent shape at the top, such as a square-top clasp.

One ball perle cotton, size 8, in color to match background bead color

Beading needles, size 10 or 12 and size 13 or 15

Beading thread, size 0, in color to match background beads, or size 15 seed beads

Sewing thread to match clasp or lining

Two 4" x 5" pieces of silk (for lining)

Pins to hold lining in place while stitching

A small box or basket to hold the ball of thread and beads when moving them down the thread.

A magnetic board with a transparent ruler, or something similar, to keep track of which row you are on while stringing beads

Thin wire

Ultra suede

Tacky glue

Toothpicks

■ Abbreviations

KB: Knit bead
PB: Purl bead
K2tog: Knit two stitches together
P2tog: Purl two stitches together
Inc1: Increase by knitting or purling (corresponding to the row) into the front and back of the stitch. Slip the stitch off the left needle.
Psso: Pick up the second stitch on the RIGHT needle and pull it over the first stitch on the needle and off the needle. This is a decrease.
Add 2 stitches: Place two loops on the end of the row as in a simple cast on.

Beginning at Row 59 on the design chart, string beads onto #8 perle cotton, always starting on the side with the black row number. The magenta number indicates the number of beads in the row, so count your beads after each row to make sure the number is the same as the magenta number for each row. At the end of each row, string on a small piece of paper (about ³⁄₈" square). This helps keep track of the rows. It is torn off as you get to it while knitting.

On size 0000 needles, cast on twenty-two stitches (two-handed cast on).

ROW 1: Knit

ROW 2: Inc1, P20, inc1

ROW 3: Inc1, K22, inc1

ROW 4: P4, PB18, P4

ROW 5: Inc1, K2, KB21, K1, inc1

ROW 6: Inc1, P1, PB24, P1, inc1

ROW 7: Inc1, K1, KB27, inc1

ROW 8: Inc1, PB30, inc1

ROW 9: Inc1, KB33, add 2 stitches

ROW 10: Inc1, P1, PB34, inc1

ROW 11: Inc1, K37, inc1

ROW 12: P2, PB38, inc1

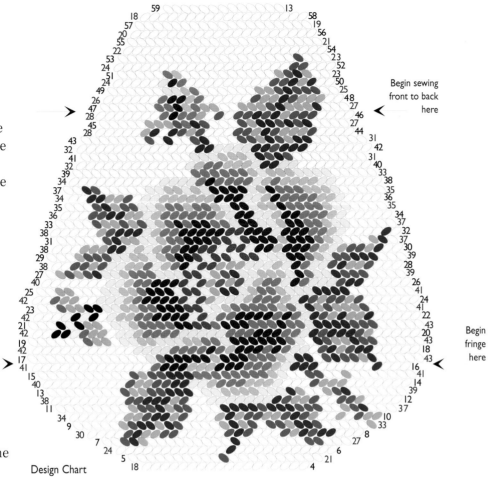

Begin sewing front to back here

Begin fringe here

Design Chart

ROW 13: K2, KB39, inc1

ROW 14: P2, PB40, inc1

ROW 15: K2, KB41, inc1

ROW 16: Inc1, P1, PB41, P1, inc1

ROW 17: K2, KB43, K2

ROW 18: P3, PB42, P2

ROW 19: K2, KB43, K2

ROW 20: P3, PB42, P2

ROW 21: K2, KB43, K2

ROW 22: P3, PB42, P2

ROW 23: K3, KB41, K1, K2tog

ROW 24: P2, PB42, P2

ROW 25: K3, KB41, K2

ROW 26: P3, PB40, P3

ROW 27: K2tog, K2, KB39, K3

ROW 28: P2tog, P2, PB38, P3

ROW 29: K3, KB39, K2

ROW 30: P3, PB38, P1, P2tog

ROW 31: K3, KB37, K1, K2tog

ROW 32: P2, PB38, P2

ROW 33: K3, KB37, K2

ROW 34: P3, PB36, P3

ROW 35: K2tog, K2, KB35, K3

ROW 36: P2tog, P2, PB34, P3

ROW 37: K3, KB35, K2

ROW 38: P3, PB34, P3

ROW 39: K2tog, K2, KB33, K3

ROW 40: P2tog, P2, PB32, P3

ROW 41: K2tog, K2, KB31, K3

ROW 42: P3, PB32, P2

ROW 43: K3, KB31, K3

ROW 44: P2, psso, P1, psso, P1, psso,

P1, PB28, P4

ROW 45: K2, psso, K1, psso, K1, psso, K1, KB27, K2

ROW 46: P2, PB28, P1

ROW 47: K2, KB27, K2

ROW 48: P2, psso, P1, PB26, P2

ROW 49: K2, psso, K1, KB25, K2

ROW 50: P2, psso, P1, PB24, P2

ROW 51: K2, psso, K1, KB23, K2

ROW 52: P2, PB24, P1

ROW 53: K2 KB23, K2

ROW 54: P2, psso, P1, PB22, P2

ROW 55: K2, psso, K1, KB21, K2

ROW 56: P2, psso, P1, PB20, P2

ROW 57: K2, psso, K1, KB19, K2

ROW 58: P2, psso, P1, PB18, P2

ROW 59: K2, psso, K3, KB13, K2, K2tog

ROW 60: P2, psso, P16, P2tog

ROW 61: Cast off

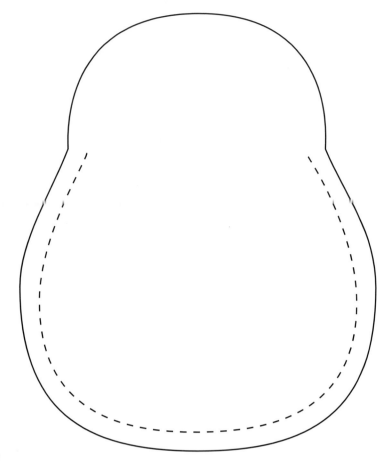

Figure I

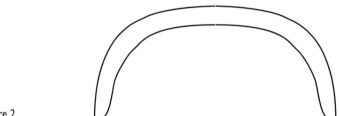

Figure 2

■ Back

Transfer six strands of light blue size 11° seedbeads onto #8 DMC perle cotton. Knit the same as for the front, counting the proper number of beads for each row before knitting each row.

■ Blocking

Wet the knitting with cold water. Blot out excess water with a dishcloth or towel. Check that all the beads are on the front of the piece and adjust as needed. Lay the piece right side up on a cookie sheet and let dry in a warm place. (I turn on my gas oven to 200°, then turn it off after it has warmed up, and place the cookie sheet in there overnight.) Sew in all loose thread tails.

■ Assembly

Pin front to back with the right sides together. Backstitch seam, beginning at Row 47 and continuing around the bottom of the bag and back to Row 47 on the other side. Be careful to leave no gap of beads in the seam. Turn to front and backstitch again, closing seam completely.

■ Sewing Bag to Clasp

Using a thin wire, temporarily attach the center top of the bag to the center of the clasp. Beginning at one

side of the clasp, backstitch bag to clasp through clasp holes. Hold the bag so that the edge of the beads are flush with edge of clasp. Repeat for other side of bag. Remove wire.

■ Lining

Lay bag on Fig. 1 Lining Pattern and check to be sure that the lining is about the same size as the knitted bag. Adjust if necessary, then cut two silk lining pieces from the Lining Pattern. Use a small running stitch to join the lining sides and bottom

Detail of inside of Wild Rose Clasp Purse

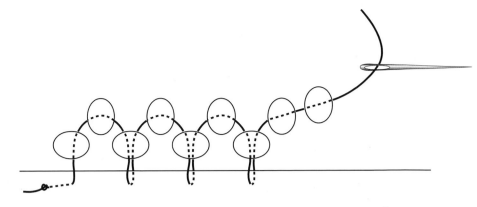

Figure 3

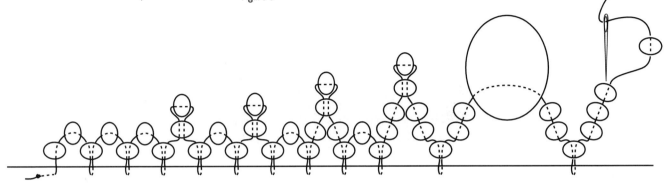

Figure 4

together. Fit into bag. Turn under and pin top of lining flush with the edge of the bag. Stitch lining in place through clasp holes.

■ Finishing

Cut two ultra suede pieces using Fig. 2 pattern. Tie a small knot in size 0 beading thread and anchor it on the wrong side of the suede. Stitch beads in a picot edging as shown in Fig. 3 on the inside curve of one of the suede pieces. Be careful not to straighten out the curve of the suede as you stitch on the beads.

On the other suede piece, begin in the same manner by stitching the small picot edging up to the curve, then gradually increase the number of beads in each picot to the center drop bead. See Fig. 4. Decrease on

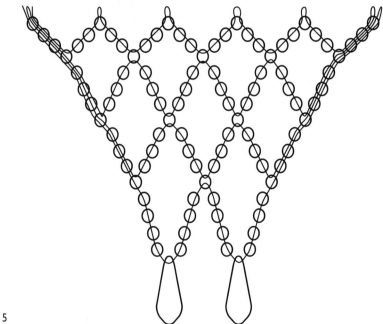

Figure 5

the other side exactly the same as the increases.

With a toothpick, carefully cover the inside of the clasp with tacky glue and press beaded suede in place.

■ Fringe

Attach 6' of beading thread at Row 16 of the knitting in the seam. Follow Fig. 5 and the directions below for the fringe.

String once:

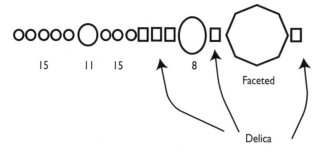

String eight times, then string above pattern once more:

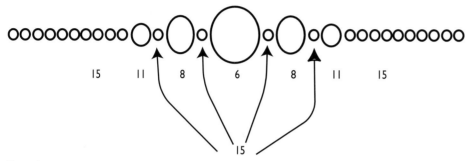

Figure 6

ROW 1: String seven size 15° beads. Take a small stitch in the seam of the knitting, three beads away. Repeat sixteen more times or to the other side of Row 16 of the knitting.

ROW 2: PNBT the last four beads in Row 1. *String seven size 15° beads, PNT the middle bead in the next loop of Row 1.* Repeat between asterisks to the end of the row.

ROW 3: PNBT the three beads in Row 1 up to the knitting. Take a small stitch in the seam and PNBT the same three beads and through the next bead in Row 1 and the next four beads in Row 2. *String seven size

15° beads and PNT the center bead in the next loop of Row 2.* Repeat between asterisks to the end of the row.

ROW 4: Repeat in the same method as for Row 3. String four size 15° beads, one dagger, and four size 15° beads for each loop in the row. Knot and weave in end.

■ Chain

Knot a 3' strand of beading thread to one loop on the clasp. String beads following Fig. 6. Knot thread through other loop of clasp. Weave in ends.

Butterflies and Snakes Crocheted Picture Frame

Elizabeth Gourley

Frame your loved ones with delicate beads in a splash of color! This frame is perfect for wallet-size photos. These instructions assume that you already know how to crochet. The whole piece is done in single crochet. If you don't know how to crochet, it will be easy to learn from any "how to" crochet book or magazine.

The finished piece measures 4 1/2" x 4". The opening is 1 3/4" x 1 5/8", or 2 3/8" x 2 1/8", if you don't add the front border.

MATERIALS

A piece of 1/8" thick cowhide leather about 12" x 10" smooth on one side

A small piece of 1/16"-thick maroon suede (optional)

Leather glue

One twisted wire beading needle

Steel crochet hook, size 7

DMC 100% cotton crochet thread #30

Heavy-duty leather matte knife

Eighty-eight Japanese tubular beads, lined lilac, Delica #073

Sixty-two Japanese tubular beads, dyed matte transparent red, Delica #774

10 grams Japanese tubular beads, matte light blue, Delica #862

Twenty Japanese tubular beads, semi-matte medium blue, Delica #693

Twenty-eight Japanese tubular beads, dyed opaque squash, Delica #651

Eighty Japanese tubular beads, black, Delica #010

Ten Japanese tubular beads, dyed matte transparent Kelly green, Delica #776

Sixteen Japanese tubular beads, lined light blue, Delica #058

4 grams Japanese tubular beads, lined pale yellow, Delica #053

Eight Japanese tubular beads, lined topaz, Delica #065

Forty-eight Japanese tubular beads, lined peach, Delica #054

Sixty-four Japanese tubular beads, Ceylon light yellow (off-white), Delica #203

Thirty-two Japanese tubular beads, opaque yellow, Delica #721

2 grams Japanese tubular beads, lined root beer, Delica #087

Eighty Japanese tubular beads, matte light brown, Delica #853

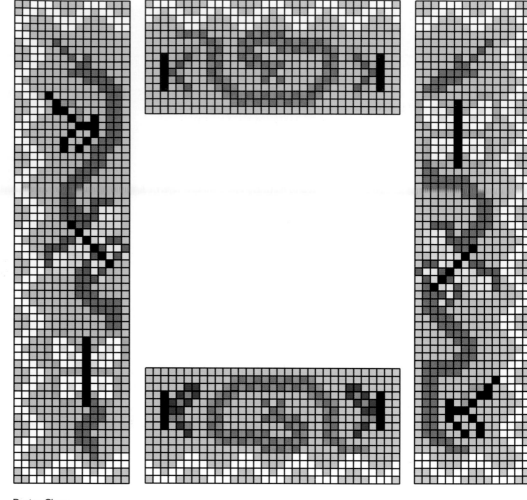

Design Chart

- ■ Semi-matte medium blue
- ▣ Matte light blue
- ▢ Lined light blue
- ▨ Matte transparent red
- ▨ Lined lilac
- ▢ Lined peach
- ■ Lined root beer
- ▨ Matte light brown
- ▨ Lined topaz
- ▢ Dyed opaque squash
- ▢ Opaque yellow
- ▢ Lined pale yellow
- ▨ Matte transparent Kelly green
- ■ Black
- ▢ Ceylon light yellow

This piece is made in four separate sections, which are glued together on the leather. Before starting each section, the beads must be strung onto the cotton thread.

■ Stringing on the Beads

It is very important to string the beads onto the cotton thread properly or the whole design will be wrong. If you string too many of a color of bead, you can easily break it off using the large needle or pliers method. If you don't have enough of a color, you will either have to start over, crochet the stitch without a bead, or cut the thread, and then add the missing bead and tie a knot. Slip bead over knot if it fits, or hide knot in back of work. Sometimes you will pick up a bead that is not quite the right color. You might be able use it if it isn't noticeable.

String the beads directly onto the ball of cotton. Using the design chart to guide you, start with the left side of the frame. This is section one. To string the beads, read the chart the opposite way from the way you read the chart to crochet the beads. String the beads from the top (Row 1 of the chart), going from left to right. Row 2 is strung from right to left.

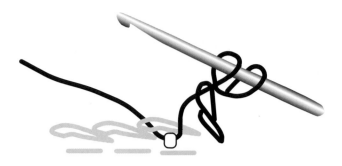

Figure 1

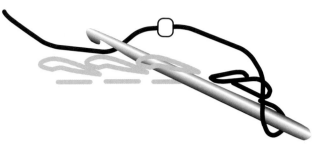

Figure 2

Row 3 is strung from left to right. Keep stringing the beads right to left, then left to right, all the way down to the bottom of the design chart.

Now you are ready to start crocheting. Make a slip knot, place the hook in the loop, and pull tight. Chain seventeen stitches.

ROW 1: Do SC in third chain from the hook. Do not use beads. SC until the end of the row. Chain two (total of fifteen stitches). Flip over work.

ROW 2: Start SC as normal by sticking hook under top of stitch (two strands) from previous row. Grab thread and pull through. You now have two loops on hook. Slide a bead down and push the bead with your fingers through the hole where you just brought the hook out. See Fig. 1. Then finish stitch by grabbing thread and pulling it through both loops on hook. Repeat this stitch until the end of the row. The beads will be on the front of the work.

ROW 3: This row is easier than Row 2 and the beads appear on the back of the piece, which is really the front. Stick hook under the top of the stitch (two strands) from the previous row. Slide a bead down until it hits the piece. Grab the thread with the hook,

making sure that the bead is caught between the hook and the piece. Then pull the thread through. See Fig. 2. Now there are two loops on the hook and the bead is attached behind the stitch. Finish the stitch by grabbing the thread and pulling it through both loops. Repeat this stitch until the end of the row.

Repeat Rows 2 and 3 all the way up, following the design chart. The last row is Row 64. Tie off the end.

Repeat for right side of frame, section 2, following the design chart.

For top and bottom of frame, sections 3 and 4, chain thirty-five stitches. Work the same as sections 1 and 2, but you will have thirty-five stitches instead of fifteen, and the last row is Row 16.

Block the sections so they lie flat.

■ Finishing

Cut two 4 1/2" x 4" pieces of 18" leather. Cut an opening in one of the pieces, 1 3/4" x 1 5/8". See Fig. 3. If you choose not to have a suede border, cut the opening 2 3/8" x 2 1/8".

Glue crocheted sections to smooth side of leather piece containing the opening. Adjust the pieces so that the edges cover all the leather,

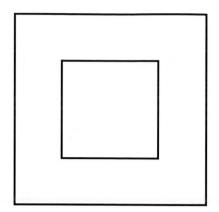

Figure 3

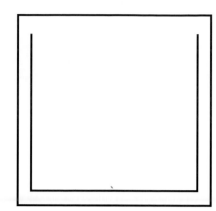

Figure 4

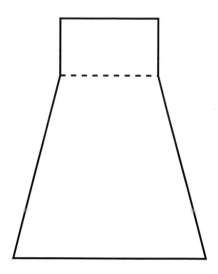

Figure 5

except around the opening, where the border goes. Line up the yellow rickrack design section to section. Cut out the suede border to fit the leather showing around the opening and glue it down. If you opted not to have the border, the crocheted sections should cover all the leather. Next, glue the two leather pieces (front and back of the frame), rough sides together. Put a line of glue along the very edge of the two sides and the bottom, leaving the top open to slide photo in and out. See Fig. 4. Using 1/8" leather and heavy-duty matte knife, cut out stand for the picture frame: 3" tall, 2" wide at base, and 1" wide at top. See Fig. 5. Score on rough side along dotted line. Glue the stand to the back of the frame with the smooth side out. Only the part of the stand above the score line is glued down. Make sure the bottom of stand hangs down 3/8" farther than the edge of frame.

Tubular Crocheted Necklace

Jane Davis

A simple crocheted cord is quickly made into an elegant showpiece by the addition of seed beads and carefully chosen accent beads.

The finished piece measures 26" long.

MATERIALS

One ball perle cotton or silk twist, size 8

$1/4$ oz or 7 grams dark transparent blue seed beads, size 8°

$1/4$ oz or 7 grams black-lined transparent AB seed beads, size 8°

$1/4$ oz or 7 grams blue-lined light blue transparent seed beads, size 8°

$1/4$ oz or 7 grams blue iris any type beads (2 cut, 3 cut, etc.), size 11°

Eleven small drop beads

Six medium drop beads

Two large drop beads

One large accent bead

Crochet hook, size 8

Clasp

Beading thread and beading needle, or wire and pliers to adhere clasp

Scissors

String the beads onto the perle cotton following Fig. 1 from left to right, 105 times. This is the first third of the necklace. Make a slip knot and chain four, sliding a bead into each chain stitch as it is made. Begin the spiral by making a beaded slip stitch into the first beaded chain stitch you made. It will be the same color bead as the bead for the current stitch. Be sure to keep the bead on the loop that the hook is through to the right of the hook, and the new bead to the right of the old bead. See Fig. 2. This will ensure that the new bead continues the spiral pattern. Continue in this manner, making a beaded slip stitch in every stitch. Every stitch you put the hook through will have the same color bead as the stitch you are making, except the drop beads.

When all the beads are crocheted, cut the thread about 3" from your work and set it aside. Onto a new length of perle cotton, string the next section of beads following Fig. 3 from top to bottom, left to right, repeating rows the number of times indicated.

Pass a loop of the new thread through the last loop of the beaded crochet cord and pull the 3" tail tight. Crochet a few stitches with the new thread and then weave the old thread into the body of your piece.

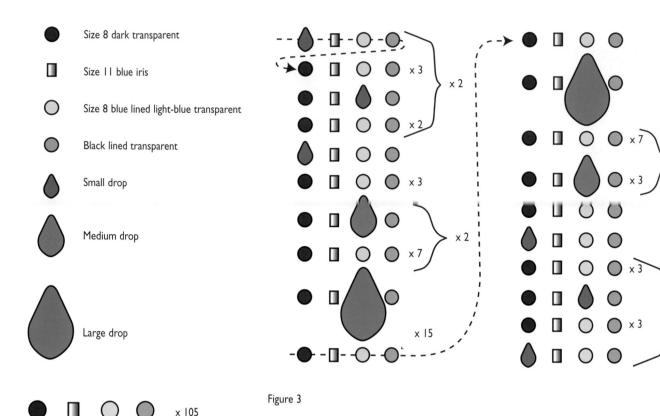

Figure 3

Legend

● Size 8 dark transparent

▯ Size 11 blue iris

○ Size 8 blue lined light-blue transparent

◔ Black lined transparent

🝊 Small drop

🝊 Medium drop

🝊 Large drop

● ▯ ○ ◔ x 105

Figure 1

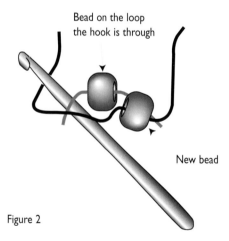

Bead on the loop
the hook is through

New bead

Figure 2

Continue crocheting until all the beads have been crocheted into the cord. Cut another 3" tail and set the cord aside. Onto a new length of perle cotton, string the final section of beads by following Fig. 1 backwards from right to left, 105 times. Attach the new thread in the same manner as before and crochet the final section of beads onto the cord. Weave in the tail threads at both ends of the necklace.

■ Blocking

Place the finished necklace in a bowl of cold water until the perle cotton is wet throughout. Gently blot excess water with a dish towel. Lay on a dry dish towel on a cookie sheet. Arrange the necklace so that all the drop beads are on the outside of the necklace in an even line. Heat your oven to 200° and then turn it off. Put the necklace in the oven overnight.

Using beading thread or wire, adhere the clasps to the end of the necklace. Using a beading thread, sew the large accent bead to the center of the necklace.

·5·

EMBELLISHMENT PROJECTS

Elephant Eloquence Necklace

Ellen Talbott

Done in the backstitch, the elephants are first embroidered on felt and then glued onto leather. Wear this necklace any time you are feeling especially wild.

The finished piece measures 8" x 11".

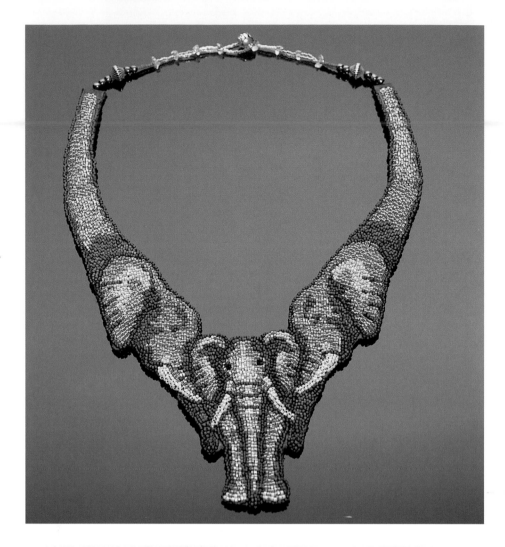

MATERIALS

10 grams Japanese tubular beads, matte metallic silver-gray, Delica #307

10 grams Japanese tubular beads, matte dark gray, Delica #306

10 grams Japanese tubular beads, transparent silver-gray luster, Delica #114

7 grams Japanese tubular beads, transparent gray iris, Delica #107

4 grams Japanese tubular beads, Ceylon gray, Delica #252

4 grams Japanese tubular beads, Ceylon light yellow, Delica #203

Ten metallic dark gray seed beads, size 6°

Two concave bicone silver beads

Eight crystal chips

One 1/2" silver rose bead

Black nylon beading thread, size D

12" x 12" medium gray felt

Thin 12" x 12" gray leather

Two beading needles, size #10

One sturdy sewing needle

Tracing paper

Glue

Scissors

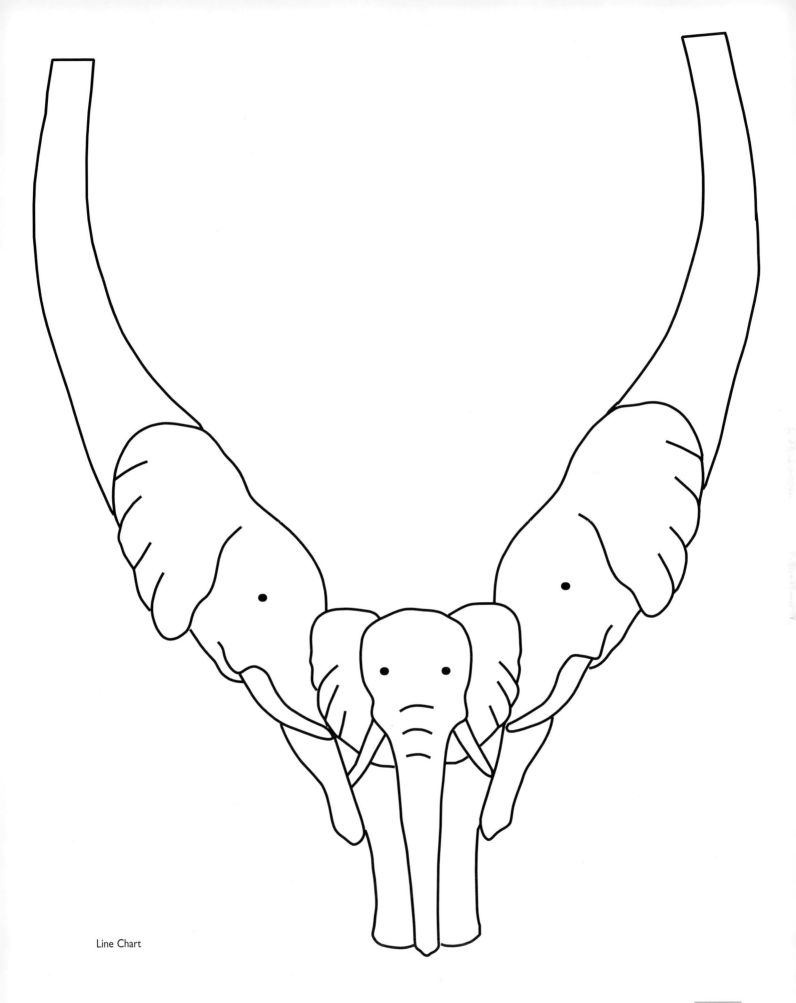

Line Chart

To do the backstitch, thread the needle with the desired length of thread and tie a knot at the end. PNUT fabric from the back side and string three beads at a time. PNDT fabric at the edge of the last bead. PNUT fabric and PNBT the last bead. See Fig. 1. When you come to a tight curve or small space, use one or two beads at a time instead of three.

Using the Line Chart, trace the outline design of the elephants onto tracing paper and pin the tracing paper onto the felt. Use a thick needle to make pinholes along the outlines. Don't make the holes too close together or the tracing paper will fall apart. Go over these holes with chalk or watercolors. This should go through the holes and onto the felt. Remove the tracing paper and draw along the dotted lines with a fabric pencil to make them more permanent.

Backstitch along the outlines with the dark gray beads, but do not outline the tusks. The tusks are embroidered with the Ceylon light yellow beads. Starting with the top of a tusk, keep your rows of beads perpendicular to the edges of the tusks. Curve the lines a bit to give the tusks a cylindrical look. Wait to do the eyes until you are embroidering the heads of the elephants.

Using the color chart as a guide, fill in all areas with the backstitch. Keep your rows fairly perpendicular to the edges of the areas. Start with the bottom of the legs of the front elephant and work your way up. Then do the trunk and head. Follow the curves of the tusks for three rows above the tusks to give an appearance that the tusks are under the skin. Do the ears by lining up the rows with the ear ruffle outlines. Next, start with the trunk of a side elephant and work your way up. Then do the other side elephant.

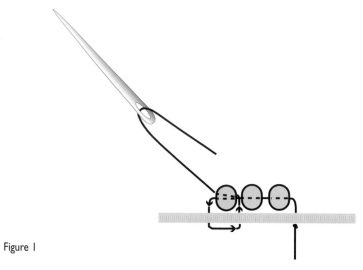

Figure I

When you are finished, cut the felt around the elephants, leaving a ¼" edge. Fold the edge to the back of the design so you can't see it from the front and glue in place. Gluing felt onto felt can be tricky if you don't have good, strong glue. You might want to use a glue gun for this. Next, glue the elephants onto the leather. When the glue is dry, cut the leather as close as you can get around the elephant design with a pair of scissors, leaving a ½" leather tab at each end. See Fig. 2. Fold the tabs in half to the front of the work and glue in place. See Fig. 3. When the glue is dry, punch a small hole into the center of the tabs with a sturdy needle ¼" from the top.

Take a length of thread about 3' long and thread each end with a beading needle. Pull one needle through the hole in the leather tab. Position the leather tab to the middle of the thread. Tie a square knot above the tab. Using both needles, string three metallic beads size 6°, one silver bicone bead, and two metallic beads size 6°. Separate the needles and on each needle string eight matte metallic silver-gray beads. Next, using both needles, string one crystal chip. *On one needle, string eight transparent gray iris. Do the same with the other needle. Then, using both needles at the same time, string on one crystal chip. Repeat from the asterisk using eight transparent silver-gray luster beads. Repeat again using eight Ceylon gray beads. Next, on one needle, string one Ceylon gray bead, five transparent silver-gray luster beads, five transparent gray iris beads, five matte metallic silver-gray beads, five transparent gray iris beads, five transparent silver-gray luster beads, and one Ceylon gray bead. Take the other needle and PNBT the beads in the opposite direction, forming a loop. Pull tight and tie the threads with a surgeon's knot. Hide excess threads down through the beads and cut.

Repeat this design on the other side, but don't form the loop. Instead, secure a ½" silver rose bead right after the last crystal chip. Hide excess thread back down through beads and cut.

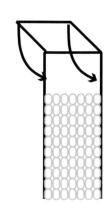

Figure 2   Figure 3

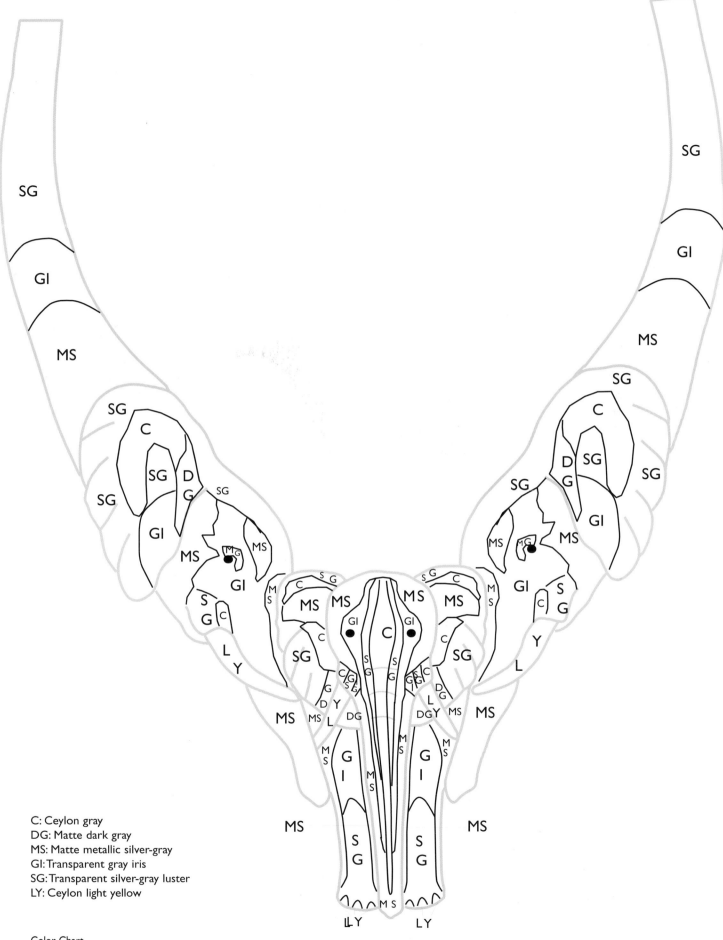

C: Ceylon gray
DG: Matte dark gray
MS: Matte metallic silver-gray
GI: Transparent gray iris
SG: Transparent silver-gray luster
LY: Ceylon light yellow

Color Chart

Ocean Artisan Mermaid Wall Hanging

Jane Davis

This piece tied for third place in the First Miyuki Delica Challenge, in 1997, and is on the cover of The Sea: Selections from the First International Miyuki Delica Challenge (edited by Barry Kahn of Caravan Beads). It was my transition piece from quilting to beading—hence, the quilting supplies used in construction. The beads are couched and backstitched on canvas.

The finished piece measures 10" in diameter.

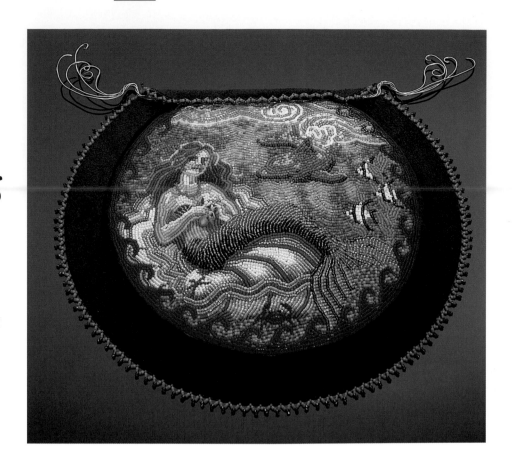

MATERIALS

½ gram Japanese tubular beads, green iris, Delica #03

2 grams Japanese tubular beads, lined peach AB, Delica #54

5 grams Japanese tubular beads, lined pale lavender, Delica #80

4 grams Japanese tubular beads, sea-foam luster, Delica #112

2 grams Japanese tubular beads, emerald gold luster, Delica #125

3 grams Japanese tubular beads, opaque chalk white, Delica #200

4 grams Japanese tubular beads, ceylon light yellow, Delica #203

2 grams Japanese tubular beads, ceylon beige, Delica #205

½ gram Japanese tubular beads, opaque salmon, Delica #206

2 grams Japanese tubular beads, opaque peach luster, Delica #207

2 grams Japanese tubular beads, opaque tan, Delica #208

5 grams Japanese tubular beads, opaque light aqua luster, Delica #217

5 grams Japanese tubular beads, white opal, Delica #220

½ gram Japanese tubular beads, lined crystal medium blue luster, Delica #243

2 grams Japanese tubular beads, lined green teal luster, Delica #275

½ gram Japanese tubular beads, luster cobalt, Delica #277

½ gram Japanese tubular beads, matte dark gray, Delica #306

½ gram Japanese tubular beads, matte metallic silver-gray, Delica #307

½ gram Japanese tubular beads, matte white, Delica #351

1 grams Japanese tubular beads, matte dark cream, Delica #353

1 grams Japanese tubular beads, silver lined teal, Delica #607

½ gram Japanese tubular beads, dyed opaque gray, Delica #652

½ gram Japanese tubular beads, dyed opaque cranberry, Delica #654

5 grams Japanese tubular beads, dyed opaque jade green, Delica #656

5 grams Japanese tubular beads, dyed opaque turquoise green, Delica #658

5 grams Japanese tubular beads, dyed opaque capri blue, Delica #659

5 grams Japanese tubular beads, dyed opaque dark mauve, Delica #662

5 grams Japanese tubular beads, semi-matte silver-lined mint green, Delica #691

1/2 gram Japanese tubular beads, transparent dark tangerine, Delica #704

5 grams Japanese tubular beads, opaque light blue, Delica #725

5 grams Japanese tubular beads, opaque dark blue, Delica #726

1/2 gram Japanese tubular beads, matte transparent gray, Delica #749

4 grams Japanese tubular beads, dyed matte transparent Kelly green, Delica #776

1 grams Japanese tubular beads, dyed transparent matte dark amber, Delica #777

2 grams Japanese tubular beads, dyed matte transparent light salmon, Delica #779

2 grams Japanese tubular beads, dyed transparent matte amber, Delica #781

1/2 gram Japanese tubular beads, matte gray/blue, Delica #792

2 grams Japanese tubular beads, dyed matte opaque sienna, Delica #794

2 grams Japanese tubular beads, matte cantaloupe, Delica #852

5 grams Japanese tubular beads, matte light brown AB, Delica #853

1 grams Japanese tubular beads, matte pale yellow AB, Delica #854

2 grams Japanese tubular beads, matte orange AB, Delica #855

1/2 gram Japanese tubular beads, matte light red AB, Delica #856

4 grams Japanese tubular beads, matte emerald AB, Delica #859

2 grams Japanese tubular beads, sparkling light green-lined chartreuse, Delica #916

2 grams Japanese tubular beads, sparkling teal-lined crystal, Delica #918

Approximately fifty teal green seed beads, size 18 or 20

Approximately thirty red-orange seed beads, size 18 or 20

Six 1/4" or smaller shells with holes for stringing

52" of 20-gauge silver wire

14" x 14" or larger cotton canvas

Scraps of thin quilt batting

White beading thread, size B

Beading or embroidery or quilting needle of your choice

Thimble

12" or larger embroidery or quilting hoop, or cross-stitch frame, preferably with a stand

Thick white glue and/or a glue gun

■ Bead Embroidery

Ocean Artisan was made with a combination of couching and backstitch, but I recommend using backstitch throughout to ensure all the beads lie flat, or to couch between every bead.

Transfer the design from the design chart onto the canvas. Stretch the canvas in the hoop. Begin by stitching beads for the mermaid's face. See Fig. 1. Pick beads carefully for details. The mermaid's mouth needs thin beads, and the beads for the eyes should be uniform.

Next, using the bead colors listed on pages 112–113, choose any section to begin and backstitch beads in place. Use the photo as a guideline for shading and the direction of the stitching. Complete each section, covering the whole surface with beads.

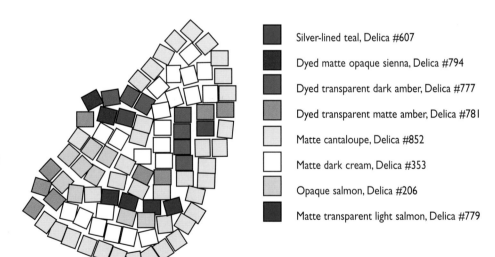

Figure 1

Silver-lined teal, Delica #607

Dyed matte opaque sienna, Delica #794

Dyed transparent dark amber, Delica #777

Dyed transparent matte amber, Delica #781

Matte cantaloupe, Delica #852

Matte dark cream, Delica #353

Opaque salmon, Delica #206

Matte transparent light salmon, Delica #779

Design Chart

Mermaid skin
  Matte dark cream, #353
  Matte cantaloupe, #852
  Dyed transparent matte amber, #781
  Dyed transparent matte dark amber, #777
Mermaid hair
  Matte pale yellow AB, #854
  Matte orange AB, #855
  Matte transparent light salmon, #779

Transparent dark tangerine, #704
Dyed matte opaque sienna, #794
Mermaid "legs" shading from light to dark
  Sparkling light green-lined chartreuse, #916
  Emerald gold luster, #125
  Lined green teal luster, #275
Mermaid fin
  Sea foam luster, #112
  Sparkling teal-lined crystal, #918
  Silver-lined teal, #607

Mermaid's shell top
  Lined crystal medium blue luster, #243
  Luster cobalt, #277
Seaweed plant on right
  Dyed opaque jade green, #656
Angel fish
  Green iris, #03
  Opaque chalk white, #200
Dolphin
  White opal, #220
  Lined pale lavender, #80

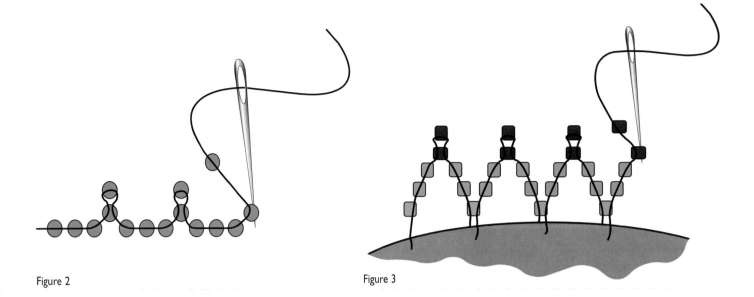

Figure 2

Figure 3

Matte transparent gray, #749
Dyed opaque gray, #652
Matte gray/blue, #792
Matte dark gray, #306
Matte metallic silver gray, #307
Crab
Green iris, #03
Dyed opaque cranberry, #654
Starfish on clam shell
Matte transparent light salmon,
#779
Clam shell
Matte light red AB, #856
Opaque peach luster, #207
Lined peach AB, #54
Ceylon light yellow, #203
Ceylon beige, #205
Opaque tan, #208
Brown AB, #853
Border
Dyed opaque dark mauve, #662
Opaque dark blue, #726
Ocean floor
Matte cantaloupe, #852
Matte light brown, #853
Ocean
White opal, #220
Lined pale lavender, #80
Semi-matte silver-lined mint
green, #691

Opaque light blue, #725
Opaque light aqua luster, #217
Dyed opaque turquoise green, #658
Dyed opaque capri blue, #659
Dyed opaque jade green, #656
Matte emerald green, #859
Dyed matte transparent Kelly
green, #776
Ocean waves
White opal, #220
Semi-matte silver-lined mint green,
#691
Lined pale lavender, #80
Sea foam luster, #112

Using the size 18 or 20 antique
beads, stitch the picot necklace. See
Fig. 2. Stitch the mermaid's necklace
in progress by making a line of six
size 18° or 20° beads above the mermaid's left hand. Then make a loop
from the top to the bottom of the
mermaid's right hand consisting of
six repeats of four beads and one
shell, then four more beads at the
end.

■ Mounting

Cut the canvas 3" larger than the
beading all around. Cut a piece of
thick cardboard into the shape of the
beading, using the outline of the
design chart as a pattern. Now, using
the cardboard as a pattern, cut a
piece of thin batting to the same size.
Sandwich the cardboard, batting,
and beading together, then glue the
3" excess canvas to the back side of
the cardboard. Cut a 1/2" x 12" strip
and a 10" circle of leather. Hot-glue
the strip around the edge of the canvas, just touching the edge of the
beading. Hot-glue the cardboard side
of the beaded piece to the center of
the 10" leather circle. Roll the top
side of the 10" leather circle down
over the top of the piece and hot-
glue in place. Make a picot edging
around the leather. See Fig. 3. Cut
the 20-gauge wire into four pieces
about 14" long. Twist together and
thread through the loop of leather at
the top of the piece. Make a bend in
the wire at each end of the leather to
hold the hooks for hanging. Then
separate the wires slightly, curling
them up and around as in the photo.

Bird of Paradise Leather Book Cover

Elizabeth Gourley

Beads on leather produces a Western aura, and the bird of paradise design—a favorite flower of California—adds to this feeling. The great look of beads on leather has its price though: lots of broken needles! But the end result is definitely worth it. This project is done in a variation back-stitch. I call it the lazy backstitch because you use anywhere from two to seven beads for each stitch, rather than the usual one to three beads per stitch.

The finished book cover measures 10½" x 8½" and fits most mass market paperbacks.

MATERIALS

- 2 grams Japanese tubular beads, silver-lined violet, Delica #610
- 2 grams Japanese tubular beads, opaque royal blue luster, Delica #216
- 2 grams Japanese tubular beads, matte tangerine, Delica #855
- 2 grams Japanese tubular beads, dyed matte transparent watermelon, Delica #779
- 2 grams Japanese tubular beads, dyed matte transparent red, Delica #774
- 2 grams Japanese tubular beads, Ceylon light yellow (off-white), Delica #203
- 2 grams Japanese tubular beads, lined pale yellow, Delica #053

- 2 grams Japanese tubular beads, dyed opaque squash, Delica #651
- 2 grams Japanese tubular beads, opaque yellow, Delica #721
- 2 grams Japanese tubular beads, silver-lined teal, Delica #607
- 4 grams Japanese tubular beads, matte emerald, Delica #859
- 4 grams Japanese tubular beads, lined lime green, Delica #274
- 5 grams Japanese beads, emerald, size 11°
- 5 grams Japanese beads, matte emerald, size 11°
- 4 grams small bugle beads, matte emerald
- 4 grams small bugle beads, silver-lined green

- 3 grams seed bead, matte green, size 8°
- 3 grams seed bead, matte dark green, size 8°
- 10" x 12" piece of golden deer chamois
- ½ yd red cotton fabric
- 6 yds ⅛" (3mm) red ribbon
- White nylon beading thread, size D
- Several beading needles, size 10
- Tracing paper
- Mini leather punch set
- Hammer
- Leather matte knife
- Leather glue
- Pliers

Design Chart

Lined lime green

Silver-lined teal

Matte emerald

Ceylon light yellow

Lined pale yellow

Matte tangerine

Opaque yellow

Opaque squash

Matte transparent watermelon

Matte transparent red

Silver-lined violet

Opaque royal blue luster

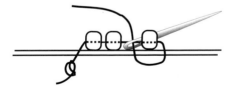

Figure 1

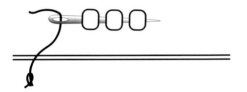

Figure 2

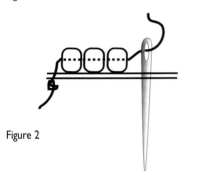

Figure 3

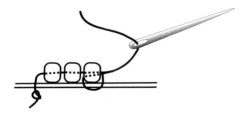

Figure 4

Note: Have plenty of needles handy for this project. Pliers will help pull the needle through the leather.

Cut a 10¹/₄" x 8" piece of chamois. Onto tracing paper, trace the bird of paradise in the design chart. Attach paper to right-hand half of chamois, with the 10¹/₄" edge as the top, by basting around the edges of the tracing paper.

Knot beading thread and pull up through the back of the piece onto the section of the outline you want to start on. String from two to seven beads, depending on the straightness of the line. The straighter the line, the more beads you use. For a curve, you would string fewer beads. PNDT leather. PNUT leather at a point between the last two beads strung. PNBT the last bead strung. See Figs. 1–4. Using the backstitch, outline the design in the Japanese tubular beads according to the design chart.

After all the outlines are beaded, carefully tear off tracing paper.

For the veins on the leaves, use the small bugle beads. The main vein runs down the center of the leaf and the secondary veins are perpendicular to the main one. The silver-lined green bugle beads are used for the front leaf, and the matte emerald

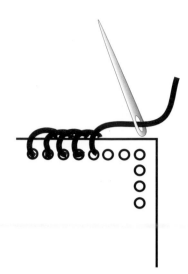

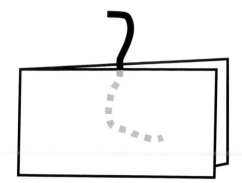

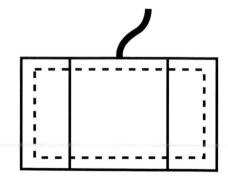

Figure 5

Figure 6

Figure 7

bugle beads are used for the back leaf. The bugle beads are strung two at a time for all veins. After you have the veins outlined, fill in the leaves with the size 11° and size 8° beads. The rows are parallel to the secondary veins. The size 8° beads will go in the middle of the veined-in areas and the size 11° beads will be used to fill in around them.

The rest of the piece (flower and stem) are done in the Japanese tubular beads. Use the backstitch to fill in all the areas with the colors according to the design chart. Place the bead rows parallel to the outline rows.

When all the embroidery is finished, punch holes about 1/8" apart all along the outer edge of the leather with a mini leather punch.

Whipstitch the ribbon through the holes. See Fig. 5. Leave about 2" ends, which will be glued under later.

■ Fabric Case (Lining)

Cut a piece of the fabric 9³/4" x 34". Fold in half with the right sides together so that the piece measures 9³/4" x 17". Pin a 14" length of ribbon in between the fabric right in the middle of the folded-in-half piece. See Fig. 6.

Sew around three edges with a 1/2" seam allowance. Don't sew on the fold edge. Make sure the ribbon inside doesn't get sewn into the seam. On the middle bottom, leave a small space open for turning the fabric right-side out.

Turn inside out and iron. Fold ends over 2³/4" and iron flat. This will form the pockets for the book's cover. Now topstitch around all the edges. This will sew the pockets down and close up the space you left open for turning the fabric.

Lay fabric flat with the pockets down. Glue leather onto the back of the fabric. See Fig. 7.

Water Lily Mirror

Ellen Talbott

This stylized water lily was inspired by the rosettes done by Native Americans. It is worked in the couching stitch.

The finished piece measures 3" in diameter.

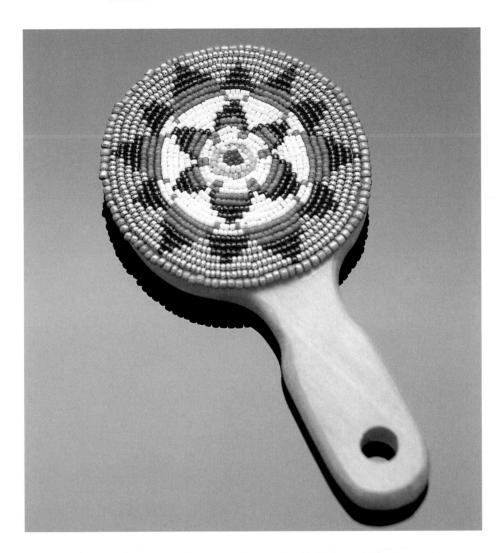

MATERIALS

Nine opaque red-orange seed beads, size 11°

Fifteen iridescent opaque yellow seed beads, size 11°

Twenty-three opaque orange seed beads, size 11°

4 grams Japanese tubular beads, Ceylon light yellow, Delica #203

1/4 oz turquoise white heart seed beads, size 11°

1/4 oz silver-lined transparent dark blue beads, size 11°

1/2 oz metallic light green seed beads, size 11°

Approximately one hundred and seven iridescent light green seed beads, size 8°

White nylon beading thread, size D

Light green felt 6" x 6"(if you use an embroidery hoop, you may need a larger piece)

Two beading needles, size 12

Round wooden or plastic 3" mirror

Scissors

Glue

Small embroidery hoop (optional)

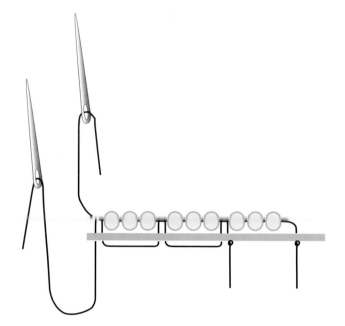

Figure 1

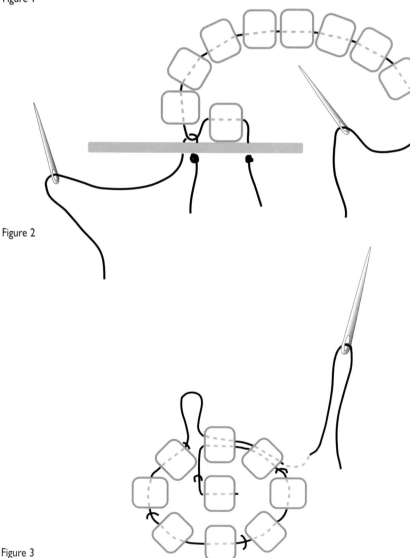

Figure 2

Figure 3

Thread two needles with separate lengths of thread and knot ends. One needle will be used to string the beads, and the other will be used to sew the beads to the felt. See Fig. 1. It is essential to keep your project flat as you work, or it won't lie flat when you're done. If this is hard for you, you may wish to use a small embroidery hoop to keep your work flat. Pull both needles up through the center of the felt. String nine red-orange beads on one needle. Sew down first bead to create the center. Arrange the other beads in a circular pattern around the center bead, sewing down the beads with the other thread between every two or three beads. See Fig. 2. To end a round, use the bead thread and PNT the first two beads in the round. Pull tight. Take the needle down through the felt and back up where next round will begin. See Fig. 3.

ROUND 2: Use about fifteen yellow beads or enough to fit around the first round. String seven or eight beads at a time. (It is difficult to predict exactly how many beads will be needed to fit around any given round, because seed beads tend to be irregular in size.) Tack down the yellow bead strand between every two or three beads. Don't forget to end this round and every round hereafter as shown in Fig. 3.

ROUND 3: Use about twenty-three orange beads. Fit around yellow round, tacking down between every two or three beads.

ROUND 4: String about thirty-one Ceylon light yellow beads and tack down.

ROUND 5: String two turquoise beads, four Ceylon light yellow beads, two turquoise beads, four Ceylon light yellow beads, two turquoise beads, five Ceylon yellow beads, two turquoise beads, four Ceylon light yellow beads, two turquoise beads, four Ceylon light yellow beads, two turquoise beads, and five Ceylon yellow beads.

When you are running low on thread on either needle, take the needle to the back of the work and tie a knot. Cut the thread from the needle. Thread the needle with a new strand of thread, tie a knot at the end, and pull the needle up from the back of the work at the same place where you left off. Continue as usual.

ROUND 6: Follow the design chart and make sure the groups of two turquoise beads line up with the groups of two turquoise beads in the previous round. Adjust the number of Ceylon light yellow beads according to the space available between the groups of turquoise beads.

ROUNDS 7–19: Follow the design chart, adjusting the number of beads for each color according to the space available.

When you have finished Row 19, cut the felt around the beads, leaving an edge of about 1/16". Be careful not to cut any threads. For the last round, use the iridescent light green beads, size 8°. String the beads and position them so they hide the felt edge. Attach the beads to the felt using the couching stitch. Bring sewing needle up through the felt at a slight outward angle and, after catching the beading thread, take the needle back down at the same angle. Finish the round and bring the needles to the back of the work. Tie a knot and trim thread ends. Glue beadwork to the back of the mirror. Place a flat, heavy object on top of the mirror to hold the beadwork in place while the glue dries.

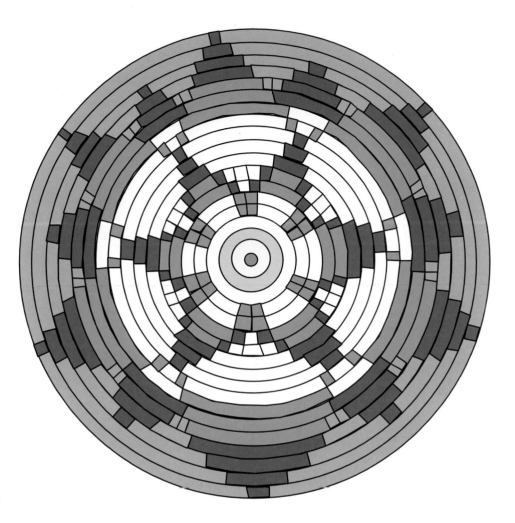

☐ Opaque orange

▨ Opaque red-orange

☐ Iridescent opaque yellow

▨ Turquoise white heart

▨ Silver-lined transparent dark blue

▨ Metallic light green

☐ Ceylon light yellow

Design Chart

Ribbons of Spring Iris Needlepoint Pillow

Elizabeth Gourley

These irises look so real you'll want to put them in a vase. This quick-and-easy project is quite a conversation piece.

The finished pillow measures 15½" x 12".

MATERIALS

15" x 20" piece of 18-count needle-point canvas
Perle cotton #8, purple
Perle cotton #8, green
Perle cotton #8, yellow
Perle cotton #8, white
Small bag of polyester stuffing
½ yd dark purple 100% cotton fabric
71 grams iridescent white seed beads, size 8°
14 grams rainbow iris seed beads, size 8°
14 grams matte lavender seed beads, size 8°

14 grams iridescent transparent lavender seed beads, size 8°
14 grams lined gold seed beads, size 8°
14 grams opaque ochre yellow seed beads, size 8°
14 grams matte translucent light green seed beads, size 8°
14 grams transparent dark green seed beads, size 8°
14 grams iridescent opaque light green seed beads, size 8°
Sewing needle small enough to fit through bead but with an eye big enough for perle cotton
Sewing and embroidery scissors

I worked on the flowers and ribbons first so that I could mindlessly fill in the white background, which uses the most beads. Using the green cotton thread, start needlepointing on the bottom stems. Make a basic sewing knot on the end of the thread. PNUT a hole of the needlepoint canvas towards the middle of the bottom of the canvas. String a dark green bead. PNDT the second hole directly above hole you came out of. See Fig. 1. PNUT a hole that is two away from the hole you first PNUT. String a dark green bead. PNDT the second hole directly above the one you just came out of. Use design chart for bead color placement.

Continue needlepointing entire piece, changing thread to match

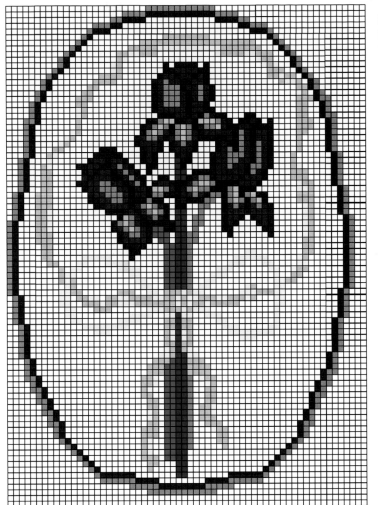

Design Chart

	Ochre yellow
	Lined gold
	Rainbow iris
	Matte lavender
	Iridescent transparent lavender
	Iridescent white
	Transparent dark green
	Translucent light green
	Opaque light green

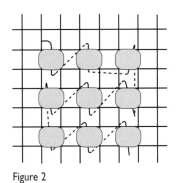

Figure I

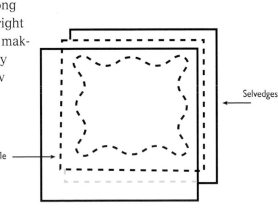

Figure 2

bead color. Make sure you skip every other hole so that the beads are not crowded together. See Fig. 2. Each bead has a nine-hole space.

When you are finished needle-pointing, cut away the needlepoint canvas from around beads, leaving a 3/4" canvas edge all the way around. Now block the piece.

From the purple fabric, cut two 11" x 14" squares for the body of the pillow. For the ruffle, cut 4"-wide strips. Sew 4" strips together to make one 100"-long strip.

In the exact middle of one of the fabric squares, pin on the beaded needlepoint canvas. Tuck under excess canvas and, using the blind stitch, sew by hand all the way around the beaded canvas. Make

sure the needlepoint canvas is tucked up under the piece far enough so that none shows.

Fold in half lengthwise the 4" strips (wrong sides together) to create 2" strips. Iron flat. Gather the selvage edges. Pin on the right side of one of the fabric squares all along the edge. See Fig. 3. Place the right sides of both squares together, making sure the gathered strips stay between both squares. Pin. Sew along edge, leaving a 1/4" seam allowance. Leave a 4" hole for turning the pillow inside out and stuffing. After it is turned inside out and stuffed, sew up the 4" hole using the blind stitch.

Selvedges

Ruffle

Figure 3

Inspirational Gallery

Antique netted Native American powderhorn. From the collection of Ellen Talbott.

Antique needlepoint purse with glass and metal seed beads. From the collection of Corinne Loomer.

Antique purse. Tambour stitch on fabric. From the collection of Suzanne Mayfield.

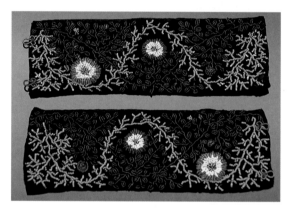

Antique embroidered cuffs. Size 18° seed beads on velvet. From the collection of Ellen Talbott.

Antique beaded purse with celluloid clasp. Done in the tambour stitch. From the collection of Corinne Loomer.

Turn-of-the-century Norwegian costume. Embroidered bugle beads and seed beads on wool. From the collection of Marit Powell.

Antique purse. Three-cut metal seed beads embroidered on fabric. From the collection of Ellen Talbott.

Antique beaded purse done in the tambour stitch. From the collection of Ellen Talbott.

Iris purse from France (1918). Tambour stitch on leather. From the collection of Mr. and Mrs. Joe Hernandez.

Antique clasp purse. Silk petit point insert with couched, beaded background. From the collection of Corinne Loomer.

Netted handbag from 1919. From the collection of Ellen Talbott.

Netted collar from Panama.

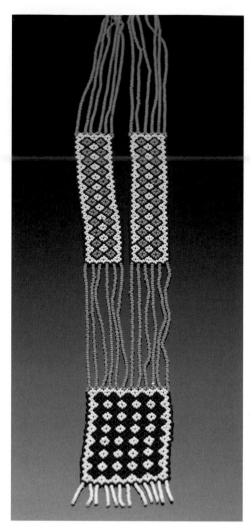

Netted necklace made in Mozambique.

Netted Zulu love letter. Zulu girls bead these "letters" to send to their lovers. Every bead color or combination of colors holds a different message.

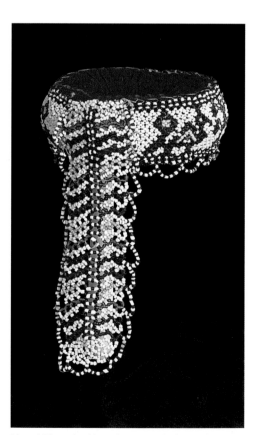

Netted African headdress for carrying baskets and jars.

Antique netted Chinese tassel. From the collection of Ellen Talbott.

Zuni Indian beaded figures "Storyteller." Done in tubular peyote stitch with netted skirts.

Zuni Indian beaded figures on horses. Done in the tubular peyote stitch.

Huichol gourd bowl from Mexico. Lined with beeswax to anchor the beads.

Couched baby moccasins. Made by the Blackfoot Indians of Montana.

African beaded tin cup. Done in a netting stitch.

African beaded doll. Various bead techniques used including netting, peyote, herringbone, and winding strings of beads around a core.

Zuni Indian beaded figures. Done in tubular peyote stitch with netted aprons.

African beaded fertility doll. Various bead techniques used including couching, netting, and winding strings of beads around a core.

GLOSSARY

Amulet: Also called a charm or fetish. An object (plant material, stones, or metal) sometimes marked with symbols or words that has magical powers. These powers protect its owner from evils, such as disease or sorcery, or they can attract good luck.

Antique beads: A brand of Japanese glass beads with large center holes and a tubular shape. The size 11° antique bead is similar to a size 13° seed bead. It also comes in a 3.3mm size, which compares to a size 8° seed bead. Antique bead also refers to any bead not currently manufactured.

Backstitch: An embroidery stitch used to sew a string of beads onto fabric or leather. Two or three beads are strung on at a time and a stitch is made to secure them to the fabric or leather. Then the thread is brought back through the last bead strung.

Bead: A bead is a small pierced object used for stringing onto a thread, string, or wire. The word *bead* is derived from the Old English words *bed* and *gebed*, which mean prayer, and the Middle English word *bede*, which means prayer.

Beading needle: A thin, straight needle 1¼"–3" long with a long, narrow eye. It is made as thin as possible so that it can pass through the small holes of beads.

Bi-cone bead: A bead that is cone-shaped at either end.

Big eye needle: A beading needle with an eye that is as large as the whole center section of the needle. The long center eye makes threading the needle very easy.

Blocking: A wetting and drying process that is done to knitted, crocheted, or needlepoint projects in order to shape them, smooth-stitch irregularities, and flatten curling edges.

Brick stitch: A beading technique that gets its name from the appearance of the beads in the finished work, which resembles a brick wall. This stitch was frequently used by the Commanche Native Americans and, thus, it is sometimes called the Commanche stitch.

Bugle bead: An elongated tubular glass bead ranging in size from ⅛"–2" long. It can be straight or twisted and comes in the colors and finishes of a seed bead.

Cathedral bead: A bead made of clear glass. Also called a transparent bead.

Ceylon: A shiny pearlized finish on an opaque bead.

Charlotte bead: A seed bead usually size 13 that has one hand-cut facet.

Conterie: An old word meaning "glass bead." It is derived from the Latin word *comptus*, which means "adorned," and the Italian word *contare*, which means "to count."

Couching: A type of appliqué work where a string of beads is appliquéd or sewn onto fabric or leather. Two needles are used in this technique. The beads are strung onto the thread with one needle and sewn down to the fabric with the other.

Delica beads: A brand of cylindrical glass beads with large center holes that make them easy to work with.

They are made in Japan and come in two sizes. The size 11° are similar to a size 13° seed bead. The 3.3mm size are close to the size 8° in seed beads.

Drawn-glass bead: A bead made with the drawn-glass technique. A tube of molten glass is pulled so that it is long and thin and is then cut into small pieces or "beads." The edges are then polished smooth.

Drop bead: An accent bead in the shape of a tear drop or a pressed, or molded, shape, such as flowers or leaves. The hole is drilled either through the side at the small end of the bead or vertically through the center.

Faience bead: The first bead made with man-made materials. It was made in ancient Mesopotamia by heating quartz sand and some form of alkali or clay. This hot mixture was formed into a bead shape probably around a stick. Then the surface was glazed with a solution of soda, potash, or niter, and entirely heated again. The result was a shiny ceramic-type bead. Historians believe that the faience bead was the forerunner to glass, which is made of the same ingredients as faience except with more alkali.

Findings: Metallic objects used in jewelry making, such as earring wires, clips, posts, clasps, headpins and eyepins, hooks and eyes, chains, hair clips, brooches, and pins.

Gather: A ball of molten glass gathered onto the end of a metal rod or blowpipe.

Greasy finish: A glass bead finish that leaves a semi-opaque bead with a dirty kind of shine.

Hank: Several strands of beads tied together and sold as one unit. The number of beads per strand and strands per hank depends on the size and weight of the beads.

Herringbone stitch: An off-loom beading technique that creates a woven-looking glass fabric. It is an old African stitch from the Ndebele tribe.

Hex bead: A faceted seed bead in which the glass is not cut but is extruded through a mold, leaving the beads with five or six sides.

Iris finish: A glass bead finish that creates a rainbow iridescence on the surface of the bead. It is also called the Aurora Borealis (AB) finish when it is used on transparent beads.

Lampwork: A bead-making technique where a glass rod is heated with an open-flamed torch and worked into a bead shape, with glass embellishments sometimes added.

Lined bead: A transparent or translucent bead with a hole that is lined with silver, gold, or paint. Sometimes the hole is etched.

Loom: A frame or structure that supports the thread used for weaving beads.

Loom work: Beadwork that is done on a loom.

Luster finish: A glass bead finish that leaves the bead glossy with a whitish tinge.

Matte finish: A glass bead finish that creates a dull surface. This is done by an acid wash or a tumbling of the beads.

Micro bead: Another word for seed beads. Any glass or metal bead with a diameter of .04" to .24".

Micro bugle: A bugle bead smaller than 1/8" long.

Metallic finish: A glass bead finish that gives the bead an extremely shiny surface.

Netting: An off-loom beading technique that creates an open mesh of beads.

Off-loom work: Beadwork that is done without a loom or structure to support the thread.

Opalescent bead: A bead made of glass that has a slightly clouded appearance. Also called translucent bead.

Opaque bead: A bead made of glass that is a solid color and lets no light through.

Peyote stitch: An ancient off-loom beading technique that is also called the gourd or twill stitch. It can be made into flat, circular, or tubular objects. It creates a solid, flexible fabric of beads.

Pony bead: A bead larger than a seed or micro bead but with the same shape and usage as one. It is any seed bead size 6° or larger. It was a popular bead among the Europeans used for trading with the Native Americans of the Southwest.

Pound bead: This was the name given to small drawn-glass beads by the bead trade long ago when they were sold by weight rather than number.

Rocaille: A tiny glass bead or seed bead. *Rocaille* means "little stones" in French.

Rosette: A circular beadwork design that is common among the Native Americans. It is done with the couching stitch.

Satin bead: A bead made with satin glass, which is created by putting air bubbles in the molten glass or by fusing layers of the same color glass to the hot gather before pulling the gather into a tube. This gives the bead a deep satiny look.

Seed bead: Any glass or metal bead with a diameter of .04"–.24" Also called a micro bead.

Tambour stitch: A bead embroidery technique used on many beaded purses at the turn of the century. The beads are threaded and secured to the back side of a fabric that has been stretched over a hoop or tambour. Then a crochet hook-like needle is pushed through the fabric from the side of the fabric facing the artist and a loop of the beaded thread is pulled through. This is repeated through interlocking the loops to create a fabric with chains of thread on one side and beads on the other.

Three-cut bead: A bead with irregular cuts all over its surface.

Trade wind bead: A drawn-glass bead made in India that was used in African trades for ivory, gold, and slaves.

Two-cut bead: A bead with two or three facets on the sides.

Twisted needle: A beading needle made of a thin wire twisted together, leaving a large, collapsible eye. It does not have a sharp point and is very flexible.

Warp: The vertical group of threads stretched across a loom.

Weft: The threads of a loom that carry the beads and run horizontally across the warp threads.

White-heart bead: A two-layered glass bead with an opaque white center and a colored transparent outer layer.

Wound-glass bead: A bead made from the wound-glass technique. A glass rod is heated, then wound around a metal rod to create a bead with a hole in it when it is cooled and removed from the rod.

INDEX